*The Sexuality of Jesus*

ALSO BY WILLIAM E. PHIPPS

*WAS JESUS MARRIED?*
*The Distortion of Sexuality*
*in the Christian Tradition*

WILLIAM E. PHIPPS

# The Sexuality of Jesus

THEOLOGICAL AND LITERARY PERSPECTIVES

1817

HARPER & ROW, PUBLISHERS

*New York, Evanston, San Francisco*

*London*

# ACKNOWLEDGMENTS

Some copyright material has been reprinted with permission in this book. Revisions and expansions of essays the author has previously published are found in chapters under the same title. They are:

Chapter 7. "Blake on Joseph's Dilemma" appeared in *Theology Today,* July 1971.

Chapter 8. "D. H. Lawrence's Appraisal of Jesus" appeared in *The Christian Century,* April 28, 1971.

Library of Congress Cataloging in Publication Data

Phipps, William E     1930–
    The sexuality of Jesus.
    1.  Sex and religion--History.   2.  Jesus Christ--
Biography.   I. Title.
BL65.S4P5     261.8'3     72–78067
ISBN 0–06–066561–0

# CONTENTS

# PREFACE

THIS book is written by a critical lover of the Christian tradition for others who also have a "lover's quarrel" with what has been transmitted across two millennia. The revitalization of biblical religion will not come from uncritical lovers who see their role as defenders of church doctrine and transmitters of it unchanged. Nor will it come from unloving critics who, like strip miners of my state, exploit resources with little attention to conserving its God-given beauty.

I lament the widening communication gap between the popular and the erudite study of religion. On the one side are the unsophisticated pietists who lack the vocabulary or the motivation to examine scholarly treatments of religion, and on the other side are the theological specialists who use abstruse jargon and thereby relate primarily to their seminary-trained peers. Both groups need to recall that Jesus, the most effective communicator in the history of religions, advised the combination of wisdom with simplicity. Thus the style I have employed is for the sake of laymen who are dissatisfied with pious platitudes regarding sex but who wish to elevate sexual discussion from the cellar to the sanctuary of life. The end notes are supplied for specialists who desire to check sources of authority.

I dedicate this study to all the Ruths of my family—mother, sister, nieces, and daughter—who have found or hopefully will find husbands as kind as the one known by their biblical namesake.

*Davis and Elkins College*                                        BILL PHIPPS
*Elkins, West Virginia*

7

# INTRODUCTION

## *Jesus, Religion, and Sexuality*

CURRENTLY there is an auspicious revival of interest in the figure of Jesus. Many long-haired and sandal-shod youth seem to identify with the appearance as well as the teaching of that ancient Jew. They are "turned on" by his personal values of compassionate love, joyous freedom, individual dignity, inclusive brotherhood, natural simplicity, and internal peace. Moreover, they admire his scathing attack on materialism and hypocrisy as well as his fearless criticism of the establishment.

The meteoritic success of *Jesus Christ Superstar* in album and on the stage is symptomatic of what a leading international news magazine has featured as "The Jesus Revolution."[1] A question from that rock opera, "Jesus Christ, who are you?" which was also on the lips of the persons whom the historical Jesus confronted, continues to tantalize the present generation. This is evoked by the bewilderment of *Superstar*'s Judas over his leader's acceptance of Mary Magdalene. He is mystified that Jesus would allow a woman of ill repute to stroke and kiss him. In that rock opera it is significant that only a woman, Magdalene, treats Jesus with full respect. It is evident that its composers wanted to underscore some of the qualities of Jesus' humanizing sexuality.

Theologians are also beginning to face up to the need for dealing with the full-orbed personality of Jesus. In an important study of Christology, Anglican Bishop J. A. T. Robinson has recently provided evidence to support this proposition: "The real difficulty for many is to admit that Jesus had *any* sexuality—*and was therefore a normal human being.*"[2] Catholic scholar Joseph Blenkinsopp, in the context of discussing Jesus' sexuality, confesses: "Christian theology has never, despite enormous efforts, found a satisfactory way of presenting the humanity of Jesus."[3] This neglect by Christians is exemplified in the so-called Apostles' Creed, which has only a comma separating Jesus' birth from his death. Yet it was the quality of Jesus' *life* that made his death redemptive: thousands were crucified in Palestine during the century in which Jesus lived.

It has been especially difficult for Christians to understand and deal with the emotions of Jesus. The first "scandalous" matter Christians were asked to explain was the horrendous suffering of God's Messiah.[4] Theologians from apostolic times onward have given considerable attention to explaining why it was necessary for the Son of God to be a "man of sorrows," and have converted into an asset what early critics of Christianity denounced. Unfortunately, little effort has been made to interpret some other facets of Jesus' emotional life. Indeed the "passion of Jesus" has come to mean exclusively his agony during the "Passion Week" that was climaxed in his crucifixion. Yet the Jesus revealed in the Gospels was a passionate person in other ways.

Jesus occasionally exploded with anger when encountering adversaries. To some Pharisees who were scornful of his Sabbath healings, he is reported as having reacted in this manner: "He looked around at them with anger, distressed by their callousness."[5] When he frequently exclaimed, "Woe unto you, scribes and Pharisees, hypocrites!" and when he "drove out all who sold and bought in the temple," he was thoroughly indignant.[6] Yet the church has tended to caricature Jesus as the "meek and mild" lamb whose full viewpoint is expressed in these words of the Sermon on the Mount: "Whoever is angry with his brother shall be liable to judgment."[7] Jesus' anger has been muted in the Christian tradition principally because some of the church fathers glorified passionlessness, an ideal which they received from Stoicism.

### THE SEX AND RELIGION MUDDLE

Sexuality is another area fraught with human passion, which has been even less related to Jesus than anger. The term sexuality is itself an emotionally charged word that needs defining here. Throughout this study it will be used broadly to embrace all affectional conduct. Thus Jesus' sexuality is his life as related directly or indirectly to the entire gamut of male-female relations. As with anger, Jesus vis à vis sexuality is often anxiously dismissed with a comment from the Sermon on the Mount which demonstrates, at least to the person supplying the proof-text, that he was against it. There, according to the customary translation, Jesus proclaims: "I say to you that every one who looks at a woman lustfully has already committed adultery with her in his heart."[8]

Many scholars and literary men have assumed that if the Gospels have anything to say regarding sexuality, it is altogether negative. For example, the distinguished historian Jacob Burckhardt has written: "Sensual enjoyment is a direct contradiction of Christianity. . . . Asceticism and its complete realization in the monastic life is the New Testament taken literally."[9] Similarly George Bernard Shaw stated: "Christianity began with a fierce attack on marriage; and to this day the celibacy of the Roman Catholic priesthood is a standing protest against its compatibility with the higher life."[10] That Irish bachelor also asserted that "the mere thought of Jesus as a married man is felt to be blasphemous by the most conventional believers; and even those of us to whom Jesus is no supernatural personage . . . feel that there was something more dignified in the bachelordom of Jesus."[11]

Assessments such as these illustrate a confusion about the relationship of sex and religion that is world-wide and history-long. It is a commonplace assumption in many cultures that the truly spiritual person censures the sensuous life. From the American Indian shaman to the Asian Indian guru, cultic taboos have been erected to discourage those who have saintly aspirations from satisfying their fleshly appetites. Why has this been the case?

In order to protect the human infant, nature's most prolongedly helpless creature, mores have evolved in every culture which curtail sexual irresponsibility. Human survival has necessitated some fidelity of parents to one another while their offspring are being nurtured. Consequently, primitive and civilized cultures around the globe have placed a positive valuation on disciplining sexual impulses. Contrary to the views of some extreme relativists, total promiscuity is a fiction. Anthropologist Ralph Linton gives a representative judgment of contemporary scholars in his field when he writes: "Different societies do differ more in their attitudes toward sex than any other activity within the field of ethics, but all of them have very definite rules governing sex behavior."[12]

Virtually all significant religious leaders have encouraged members of their faith to avoid illicit and violent means of sexual expression. Although cultists have occasionally arisen who encouraged licentiousness, this is not characteristic of the mainstream of world religions. The danger is rather the opposite: religious leaders have customarily had such a strong sense of rectitude that, in opposing those whose sexual discipline is lax, they have often become excessively stringent and proscriptive. This can be illustrated by looking briefly at several notable leaders.

Twenty-five centuries ago Mahavira founded the Jain religion which has continued to the present day in India. According to one tradition he was a lifelong celibate, but according to another he left his wife and daughter at the age of thirty. Mahavira's coital abstinence was associated with his contempt for the opposite sex. This is the way he condemned women: "The greatest temptation in the world is women. . . . Men say, 'These are the vessels of happiness,' but this leads them to pain, to delusion, to death, to hell, to birth as hell-beings or brute beasts. . . . They should not speak of women, nor look at them, nor converse with them, nor claim them as their own." Because of this outlook of their leader, one of the basic vows of the Jainist ascetic (though not of lay members of the sect) is: "I renounce all sexual pleasure."[13]

The life of Siddhartha the Buddha, a contemporary of Mahavira, is another case in point. The prince was married at sixteen to a beautiful girl and lived with her for a decade before chancing to see the miserable plight of ordinary humanity. Then, after encountering a monk by whose serenity he was much struck, he decided that he might also find freedom for himself—and for mankind—through release from secular ties. At that time he was told that his wife had given birth to a son. The news precipitated the bitter response: "A fetter has been forged." Deciding to break away from this impediment, Buddha left his wife and infant to be cared for by his royal father and retreated to a forest hermitage. On that same night it came about that he saw some dancing girls "with their dress fallen apart so as plainly to disclose their nakedness" and that exposure "further increased his aversion for sensual pleasures."[14] For the remainder of his long life he avoided the opposite sex as much as he could.

Mahatma Gandhi shared many of the same beliefs about sex as Mahavira and Buddha, in his Indian culture. He admitted remorsefully that he married and became a father before gaining the mature insight that the pure and healthy life required coital renunciation. Gandhi maintained sexual continence from 1906 onward (for more than half his life) even though he continued to live in the same household with his devoted wife, whose consent to this arrangement he had first obtained. He advocated celibacy for everyone, claiming that those practicing it would be energized with strength from God.[15]

Mary B. Eddy, the founder of the Christian Science church, believed that physical sexuality was metaphysically unreal. While admitting that coitus is a present necessity when a child is desired, she speculated that it might be unnecessary even for reproduction after science discovers how all people can, like Jesus, be conceived parthenogenetically.[16] She envisaged this evolution: "Proportionately as human generation ceases, the unbroken links of eternal, harmonious being will be spiritually discerned." As humans become less enmeshed in the fleshly they will realize that "man is not matter; he is not made up of brain, blood, bones, and other material elements."[17] Although Mrs. Eddy was married three times and was a mother, she favored celibacy as the truly spiritual life-style.

What is the prevailing situation now regarding sexuality among Christians? Masters and Johnson have recently supplied clinical evidence to demonstrate that "the factor of religious orthodoxy still remains of major import . . . in almost every form of human sexual inadequacy."[18] It is characteristic, so they have found, for persons with a strong religious background to have internalized many negative exhortations but to have had little positive training in the area of sexuality. In evaluating that study from the standpoint of Protestantism, theologian Seward Hiltner reluctantly admits, "Sex is and may remain an ecclesiastical ostrich."[19] Sex and religion are the areas most fraught with emotion, and for that reason they are the last to be exposed to rationality.

If Pope Paul VI articulates the consensus of current Roman Catholic opinion, then his pronouncements pertaining to birth control, priestly celibacy, and consecrated virginity show that his church has not modified its position significantly since the Middle Ages, the nadir for sexual attitudes and practices in Christian history. Along with the Vatican II Council, he lauds "the superiority of virginity" to marriage. The present Pope has even revived the medieval rite by which women who do not plan to join a religious order can make a permanent commitment to the virginal state.[20] In 1971 the Vatican released a survey which showed that mandatory celibacy was the main reason for the sharp increase in defections by the younger priests.[21] Nevertheless the Synod of Bishops, which met at the Vatican later that year, voted to join their pope in supporting the status quo. Paul VI has also reinforced his church's traditional position in asserting that marriage is honorable for those who lack the temperament for lifelong celibacy, but only if its chief purpose is baby production and not love-making.

It appears that the church has become severed from her historical Jewish moorings with respect to sexuality and has been nearly capsized by some perennial pagan perspectives that debase the physical and emotional aspects of life. In the name of the one who compared the spiritual life to a wedding celebration, overt sexual expression has been, more often than not, tolerated grudgingly as a concession to the weakness of the flesh. Many members of our increasingly depersonalized society have not heard the good news that the Man of Nazareth was both emotional and rational.

Little wonder then that many youth who are alienated by the omnipresent technocracy of the Western world are also rejecting the "pale Galilean" transmitted to them by their elders and are finding fresh and vital the Jesus who is portrayed in the Gospels. There it is seen that his intuitive life, like Wordsworth's poetry, was a "spontaneous overflow of powerful feelings." The youthful glossolalists from Protestant and Catholic backgrounds who claim they are getting "high" on Jesus serve to point up the need for conventional churchgoers to integrate more uninhibited ardor into the routine order of their worship and life-styles. Jesus' pattern of life contained a Dionysian as well as an Apollonian element, and that full and wholesome life is now being rediscovered.

The derogatory outlook toward sexuality held by some Eastern and Western religions is not intrinsic to all religious phenomenon.

That this is true can be seen in the dominant perspective of ancient Judaism. Although that religion was affected by some sexual attitudes which may well be evaluated as less than ideal, it nevertheless stands out in that it has enthusiastically sanctioned the physical and mental aspects of sexuality. Apropos here is Rabbi Abba Silver's observation: "The renunciation of normal sex life was never regarded as a virtue in Judaism. This is one of the marked differences which distinguishes Judaism from most of the classic religions of mankind."[22]

As an example of the ancient Jewish outlook on sexuality it is instructive to study the life of Jesus. Jewish scholar David Flusser has pointed out that with the exception of the historian Flavius Josephus and possibly the apostle Paul, more is known about Jesus than about the life of any other ancient Jew living in post–Old–Testament times.[23] But more: Jesus' life-style has made so indelible an impact on most world cultures that it merits close study even apart from ethnic ties. Rabbi C. G. Montefiore has referred to Jesus as "the most important Jew who ever lived, one who exercised a greater influence upon mankind and civilization than any other person, whether within the Jewish race or without it."[24]

The personality of Jesus—like that of other creative geniuses in religion—should not be studied only as an exemplar of a cultural type, for he intensified those qualities which differentiate man from other animals in every milieu. It is recognized that he accentuated those distinctive human qualities of freedom, worship, and compassion. Perhaps he should also be admired as one who brought sexuality to full flowering. Since it is integral to man's essential being, it is not ridiculous to find *homo sexualis* as among man's many attempts at self-definition. Sexuality is not an added accretion that a person may or may not elect to have. Psychoanalysis has shown us that sexuality is not an occasional type of behavior nor, like eating, a mere organic functioning.

That sexuality is a fundamental part of human nature—physiologically *and* psychologically—is displayed in a simple but profound way by the older Genesis creation account. Although made from moist dust like the rest of the animals, man is discontinuous with them because they do not relieve his desire for a partner. Only a human of the opposite sex causes him to cry out in delight "This is it!" and to unite with her so that "the two become one flesh." That ancient writer seemed to realize that God made man the sexiest of all animals. He is well interpreted by an early Christian thus: "When God invented the plan of the two sexes, he placed in them the desire of each other and joy in union. So he put in their bodies the most ardent desire of all living things, so that they might rush most avidly into these emotions."[25] The biblical doctrine of creation held that man was a combination of flesh and the divine breath, and that no attempt should be made to curtail their proper expression. Francis Thompson's poetry captures the Hebrew's psychosomatic outlook succinctly: "In this narrow bed,/Spirit and sense are wed."

Christians have been more embarrassed than appreciative of the human sexual differentia bestowed by their Creator. Generally speaking, there has been an uneasy acceptance of such facts as the following: beasts are in heat for a season, but humans have sexual desire throughout the year; only a small fraction of human coital encounters are aimed at producing offspring; and humans may be the only animal that can experience pleasurable orgasms when unable to conceive. Eunuch Origen was cognizant of some of this comparative behavior and drew from it a quaint moral. Noticing that the lower orders tended to be less active sexually than man, he encouraged Christians to gain purity by emulating animal conduct![26] Along with other church fathers, he admired those creatures which abstain from sexual intercourse except for short inseminating periods. Most theologians since the time of Origen have likewise been reluctant to draw positive implications from the sexual facts of life.

In this book an attempt will be made to release the pivotal personality of the Bible from the dehumanizing treatment of sexuality in much of Christian tradition. I share the stance of Norman Pittenger, an Anglican specialist in Christology, who has recently written:

It is of first importance to stress that to speak of Jesus as being truly human is also to speak of him as a sexual being. Whatever ways he may have chosen to express or to re-channel his sexuality . . . it is clear that when his sinlessness is mentioned we do not, or should not, take this to imply a-sexuality. Alas, however, much Christian thinking has done just this; in consequence we have the anaemic, lifeless, almost effeminate Christ of the Victorian stained-glass windows and of some popular portraits.[27]

How does this study differ from my previous book on Jesus' sexuality? In *Was Jesus Married?* I worked like a detective with the historical issue foremost in attention. By piecing together shreds of circumstantial evidence from ancient biblical and nonbiblical sources pertaining to marital sociology in the Palestinian culture; by a fresh exegesis of passages in the Gospels appealed to by those defending the single status of Jesus; and by combining all of this with data from scrolls that archaeologists have found at Qumran and at Nag-Hammadi, I defended my hypothesis that Jesus probably married. There are Catholic, Protestant, and Jewish scholars who agree with my historical inference.[28] Since virtually every relevant historical text was scrutinized in researching that book, there is little point in probing further into Jesus' marital status. In this sequel I plan to focus on reconstructing Jesus' sexuality from data contained in Jewish and Christian documents pertaining to the first century of the Christian era. I shall also examine critically a variety of ways in which the Jesus and sexuality motif has been treated by some theologians, philosophers, and literary artists in the Christian tradition. This study is independent of the historical question of how Jesus overtly channeled his sexuality. Exploring the quality of a historical character's sexuality as seen from the perspectives of various admirers is a broader and a more important matter than ascertaining whether he had or did not have a spouse.

In the first main section of this study, sexual attitudes in general and the sexuality of Jesus in particular will be investigated from the perspective of Jewish Christianity. Attention will be on the biblical writers, nearly all of whom were Jewish. Luke is the only exception we know of, and his idioms reveal that much of his material came from Semitic sources. Although there were several subcultures in ancient Palestinian Judaism, they all encouraged tender affection and affirmed the holiness of sexual union within the bond of matrimony.

The physiology of sex begins with conception, so it is relevant to our inquiry to relate the sexuality of Jesus to that of his mother. If an ovum of Mary was not fertilized by a human, then Jesus' nature could have been qualitatively different from human nature as universally experienced. Some influential Latin church fathers maintained that it is wrong to assume that Jesus had normal sexuality because he was virginally conceived. Bishop Hilary claimed that Jesus had a special physical constitution void of sexual desire because of his miraculous generation.[29] Bishop Augustine followed this position, and consequently it became the prevailing doctrine. In his last writing he stated: "Christ had no strife of flesh and spirit which came upon human nature from the transgression of the first man inasmuch as he was born of the Spirit and the Virgin, not through fleshly desire."[30] These Gentile viewpoints will be contrasted with the perspective of the source material used in Luke's story of the virginal conception.

After ascertaining the Jewish Christian perspective on Jesus' conception, his maturation from birth onward will be looked at through the eyes of the "scribes and Pharisees." This crucial question will be investigated: to what extent was Jesus a product of his Jewish culture and to what extent was he independent of Judaism—especially with regard to his sexuality? Even though Jesus spent approximately 90 percent of his life as a private Jewish citizen out of the public eye, little attention has been given to the environmental setting for those formative years. It seems that most Christians would like to forget that Jesus and his family were devout Jews, immersed in the milieu to which they belonged. Leander Keck has recently observed that "far more needs to be done to rehabilitate the Jewishness of Jesus, not simply because good Jewish-Christian relations commend it but because the integrity of our picture requires it."[31] The meager information in the Gospels about Jesus' private life in Nazareth and public life as a rabbi will be supplemented by a substantial amount of extrabiblical documentary material pertaining to the coming of age of a student of the Torah.

The inquiry into the impact upon the maturing Jesus of the customs of his culture leads into an examination of the sexuality of the adult Jesus. This will principally involve looking at Jesus as the women of the Gospels saw him. Perhaps because most New Testament expositors have been male, the place of females in the life of Jesus has not been given due attention. Yet any man's behavior toward the opposite sex discloses much about his total outlook toward life.

The matrix for early Christian sexual morality was the Jewish ethos, but as the church gravitated westward it was infiltrated by sharply different standards. Robert Gordis describes that Hellenizing process thus: "As Gentile Christianity all but submerged the original Jewish-Christian nucleus, the Greek element triumphed over the Hebrew. . . . The most palpable illustration of this thesis lies in the area of sex and family life."[32] This shift in Christian sexual morality is prominently displayed by those scholarly churchmen who were much affected by the prevailing currents of Greco-Roman philosophical ethics. Hence, the second part of this study will examine those Christian interpreters of sexuality from non-Jewish cultures who presented Jesus as one who was dedicated to sensuous renunciation. This interpretation, as we shall see, came to a crescendo with the existentialist Søren Kierkegaard, who has exerted more influence on twentieth-century Christian theology than any other philosopher. Quite categorically he maintained that loving God implies the abandoning of all sensual attachments as Jesus allegedly did.

In order to show that Christian perspectives toward the sexuality of Jesus and his followers have not been altogether distorted, the treatment of ascetics such as Augustine and Kierkegaard has been balanced with a study of the main spokesmen of the Protestant Reformation. The Reformers were dedicated to the renewal of the apostles' doctrines, and not the least of these was that sexual desire was one of the Creator's good gifts. They dusted away some cobwebs of celibate interpretation that had obscured the New Testament's portrait of a virile Jesus.

In the post-Reformation era more attention has been given to Jesus' sexuality by literary artists than by theologians. Consequently we shall look at Englishmen William Blake and D. H. Lawrence, who fought prudery from their chronological positions in history at opposite ends of the Victorian era. They were infatuated both by Jesus and by sexuality, and attempted to establish some interrelation between them. Their general perspective was similar to that of Pittenger when he writes, "Human sexuality is intimately part of the human dynamism for self-fulfillment; and this is apparent in the experience of men and women, who at their best are not content unless in some fashion they can experience 'love' and 'self-giving' in their sexual relationships."[33]

To complete the trilogy of literary studies, the treatments of Jesus' sexuality by Blake and Lawrence will be followed by that of Nikos Kazantzakis. That eminent Greek poet and novelist, who was in sexual turmoil throughout much of his life, looked upon Jesus as the mirror image of his own ideal self. He appreciated Lawrence's perspective on sex and yet found winsome the contrasting sexual outlook of the ascetic monks of his culture. Consequently his Jesus figure is a piquant portrayal of the disharmonious sexuality of modern man.

Our study will conclude with some theological musings: In what ways should Christians attempt to imitate Jesus? Both the unrealism and the relevance of the traditional notion of Jesus as the model of morality, sexual and otherwise, will be pondered.

# I

## *Jesus' Dual Paternity*

OVER the past century there have been few matters relating to the Bible which have provoked more rancorous disputes than the question of how the earthly existence of Jesus began. Many Christians and non-Christians first became aware of the modern critical approach to the New Testament as they examined the arguments pertaining to Jesus' alleged virginal conception, commonly but less precisely called his "Virgin Birth."

It is instructive to compare the popular reactions to the literary-historical investigations of Jesus' generation and the scientific treatments of man's genesis. Until the publication of Darwin's *Origin of Species* there was a consensus in Western civilization that the birth of mankind came about a few thousand years ago with a special intervention by God in the creation of Adam and his spouse. Then came the theory of natural selection, which was heatedly debated by Europeans in the nineteenth century and by Americans in the twentieth. Out of this debate most theists came to realize that Darwin's theory was compatible with the doctrine that God created the universe. Indeed, Darwinism is not generally thought of as doing a service to religion by freeing the opening chapters of Genesis from a literalistic interpretation. There is now less emphasis on a transcendent Omnipotence who made all things in 144 hours by a series of momentous acts, and correspondingly there is more emphasis on an immanent Spirit who is perennially creative. A dual causality is now seen to be operative: God is understood to be the ultimate cause of the universe and the distinctive spirit of man, but he uses an evolutionary process for creating human life from animal organisms.

The reconciliation between science and religion is not nearly so complete with respect to the birth of the "Second Adam." The traditional theory of Jesus' conception was first intensely discussed by European scholars in the nineteenth century. Then, in a movement paralleling in time and place the debate over biological evolution, shock waves of the Christological argument reached America in the first part of the twentieth century. During the past generation the discussion has subsided, but unfortunately this is not because Christians have arrived at a general consensus on the issue. On the basis of a 1964 sociological survey, approximately half of the Protestants and three-quarters of the Roman Catholics in the United States accept as completely true the statement, "Jesus was born of a virgin."[1] Memories of harsh fundamentalism-modernism fights and a proneness to let sleeping dogma lie are more operative in this lack of discussion than general agreement. The battle lines can still be distinguished. The supernaturalists hold that Jesus was not conceived as other humans by the biological union of the sperm of a man with the ovum of a woman. This outlook is opposed by those who maintain that human reproduction occurs only when a male supplies half of the chromosomes, and that therefore Jesus was born by ordinary generation. Scientific naturalists tend to explain away the traditional birth stories as little more than pious fairy tales. They posit that Jesus must have been sired either by Joseph or by some other man or else was not a historical and human person.

A rapprochement might be accomplished between the supernaturalist and the naturalist points of view if both sides could adapt to the conception of Jesus an outlook which is commonplace among Christians with regard to the evolution of the universe and the life within it. The dynamic Spirit of God need not circumvent the natural processes in generating the world in its totality or in generating Jesus in particular.

An examination of the treatises written on the "Virgin Birth" over the past century shows that most polemicists do little more than marshal tired arguments to justify either their supernaturalist or their naturalist stance. Little progress has been made toward achieving a common understanding, since no thoroughgoing attempt has been made to understand the outlook on conception of the culture that produced the Bible. For instance, the American theologian Thomas Boslooper[2] and the German theologian Hans von Campenhausen,[3] who have written the most scholarly recent studies on the "Virgin

Birth," do not even consider a most germane ancient Jewish point of view in this matter, which might be called that of a dual paternity. In their more mystical moods the ancient Jews thought of a procreative trinity composed of God, husband, and wife. In this chapter I shall: (1) present evidence for this outlook from the Scriptures and from other Jewish tradition; (2) discuss how the New Testament nativity narratives can be harmonized with it; and (3) show how the idea became distorted in the course of early church history.

## EVIDENCE FROM ANCIENT JUDAISM

The instrumental presence of God in any human conception which he has blessed is not a new idea. The elements of "dual paternity," if one may call it that, may be found in both ordinary and extraordinary situations in Hebrew Scriptures. An illustration of the former is in Ruth 4:13: "Boaz took Ruth and she became his wife. When he had intercourse with her, the Lord caused her to conceive and she bore a son." The divine presence was considered even more significant when a wife conceived who had been thought barren. The most prominent example of such a situation is found in Genesis 21:1–2: "The Lord visited Sarah as he had said, and the Lord did to Sarah as he had promised. And Sarah conceived, and bore Abraham a son in his old age."

In some other Hebrew birth accounts the human father is implicitly assumed but not explicitly mentioned. As a way of expressing piety, it is said of Rachel and again of Leah that God "opened her womb."[4] And a Hebrew poet, without intending to deny the role of his human father, thought of God as contributing to his conception. That psalmist addressed God in this way: "Thou didst form my inward parts./ Thou didst knit me together in my mother's womb."[5]

This sense in Hebrew Scriptures of the agency of God in human events of all kinds was a product not so much of poetic fancy as of theological conviction. The Hebrews, living as they did in a pre-scientific culture, were not awed by physical causation. Although they did at times show a naïve awareness of it, they considered it relatively insignificant by comparison with divine causation. For example, in the Exodus account of the crossing of the Sea of Reeds there is mention of "a strong east wind" separating the waters. But that explanation was not so important as the affirmation regarding the Lord's action: "At the blast of thy nostrils the waters piled up."[6] Or again, in a number of biblical accounts natural causality is ignored in diagnosing disease.[7] However, it would be untrue to conclude that the Hebrews thought all sickness was directly decreed by God.

As a part of their belief in a continuously creative God, the Hebrews held that organic life could not be adequately explained in a physiological manner. Acting as a life force was one function of God's Spirit (*ruach*).[8] The Spirit produced land fertility and animal reproduction as well as human offspring.[9] Job affirmed: "The Spirit of God has made me."[10] Accordingly men were sometimes dignified as "sons of the living God."[11] The etymology of "procreation" suggests the ancient theology of generation. A *pro*creator was viewed as one who acts on behalf of the creator, just as a pronoun is a word that represents a noun.

Ancient Jewish tradition makes more explicit the theory of dual paternity suggested by Hebrew Scriptures. In the *Talmud* there is an interpretation of the first conception account of Genesis in which Eve exclaims, "I have brought a child into being with the help of the Lord." On the basis of that text this assertion is made: "There are three partners in the production of any human being—the Holy One, blessed be he, his father, and his mother."[12] According to the distinguished Jewish scholar Israel Abrahams, "the rabbinic theory of marital intercourse is summed up" in this claim that God participates as a third parent in every act of procreation.[13] A similar interpretation is given in a Genesis midrash: "Rabbi Simlai said: . . . 'In the past Adam was created from the dust of the ground and Eve was created from Adam. Henceforth it is to be "in our image and after our likeness"—meaning, man will not be able to come into existence without woman, nor woman without man, nor both without the Shekinah.' "[14] "Shekinah" is a postbiblical circumlocution for YHWH and is often used interchangeably with "Holy Spirit" (*ruach hakodesh*).[15] It means literally "the One Who Dwells Within" and thus refers to the immanent expression of God. The Shekinah is present when the devout assemble to worship[16] and among marital partners. "When husband and wife are worthy the Shekinah is with them."[17]

Philo, a Jewish contemporary of Jesus, shared with the Palestinian rabbinic tradition a belief that procreation resulted from divine-human cooperation.[18] For example, he stated that Isaac was a son of Abraham and Sarah[19] and also a "son of God" because he was begotten by God.[20] In one treatise Philo drew allegorical significance from the fact that there is no overt mention of Abraham, Isaac, Jacob, or Moses engaging in marital intercourse. He thought that this meant figuratively that the wives of those patriarchs were impregnated by God.[21]

It is seen then that ancient Jews in both of the main geographic divisions—those of Diaspora as well as those of Palestinian areas—accepted a theory of dual paternity. There is no historical indication whatever that they believed that life could be propagated without human insemination. They viewed pagan legends of unnatural conceptions as blasphemous because they ran counter to the Genesis theology of creation. The Hebrews held that the Torah's first command, "Be fruitful and multiply," was obeyed when God's blessing was coupled with the heterosexual union of those made in his image.

## EVIDENCE FROM THE NEW TESTAMENT

What do the earliest historical sources of Christianity say about Jesus' paternity? The apostle Paul brought divine and human parentage into juxtaposition: Jesus was born "of David's seed according to the flesh," yet he is also designated "Son of God."[22] In a similar manner Christians, although seminally generated, are also spoken of as "sons of God" and are thereby privileged to call God their father.[23] Paul, along with the writer of Mark and the compiler of the teaching source "Q" used by Matthew and Luke, was probably unaware of a virginal conception tradition about Jesus. If they did know of it, their neglect of mentioning it suggests that they judged it to be either false or insignificant. Since it was through Joseph that the early Christians traced Jesus' descent from David, it would have been nonsense for Paul to claim that Jesus was of Davidic descent yet was not a physical son of Joseph. No New Testament writer asserts that Joseph was only Jesus' legal or foster father.

In the Fourth Gospel Jesus is called both "Joseph's son" and "God's only son." The prologue of that Gospel affirms that each person who receives God has come into being through a cause other than the desire of a human father. All "children of God," Jesus included, are "the offspring of God himself."[24] In the dialogue between Jesus and Nicodemus, the evangelist graphically alludes to the complete life as consisting of birth by the Spirit from above in addition to natural fleshy conception.[25]

The only New Testament books that appear to state that Jesus was virginally conceived are Matthew and Luke. Matthew seems inconsistent in this testimony, since it is through Joseph that Jesus' genealogy is traced. Moreover, Jesus is referred to in that Gospel as "the carpenter's son."[26] Elsewhere I have argued that the Matthew 1:18–25 conception episode is based on a Jewish Christian tradition of dual paternity which has been obscured by a later redaction.[27] More recently Charles T. Davis, in a thorough scholarly treatment of the Matthean nativity story, has demonstrated that the earliest tradition probably contained no reference to the fulfillment of Isaiah's prophecy that "a virgin shall conceive" (1:23) and no instructions to Joseph to abstain from sexual relations with his wife (1:25).[28] The focus of this chapter will be on the nativity story of Luke, which is independent of the Matthean narrative.

The claim that the Third Gospel gives the fullest account of Jesus' virginal conception rests on six Greek words in Luke 1:34 and 3:23. Otherwise the entire writings of Luke would unambiguously support a theory of dual paternity. This is clearly seen in Luke 2:48–49 where Jesus' mother is represented as saying: "Your *father* and I have been looking for you anxiously." To this Jesus responds by claiming that he had been all along in his "Father's house." Luke does not suggest here or elsewhere that Joseph stood *in loco parentis* to Jesus. Also Luke has citizens of Jesus' home town question, "Is not this Joseph's son?"[29] Along with these assertions pertaining to Jesus' natural family are frequent references to Jesus as son of the divine Father.

In Luke 1:34 Mary is represented as inquiring after Gabriel's annunciation, "How shall this be, since I know not a man?" If "since I know not a man" is excluded from the question then Mary's puzzlement pertains to the magnificent destiny forecast in the preceding verses for a peasant's son. Mary was already betrothed to Joseph so it is unlikely that she would have been bewildered over who might become the agent of impregnation. The question would have been pointless if she was anticipating or was engaging in normal matrimonial relations with Joseph. A number of New Testament scholars have plausibly conjectured on weak textual and strong literary grounds that the allusion to virginal conception is an interpolation not contained in the written traditions that Luke used.[30]

The genealogy of Jesus in Luke 3:23 contains a parenthesis which voids the purpose of the original compiler, namely of tracing Jesus' lineage through Joseph. It reads: "Jesus . . . being the son (as was supposed) of Joseph. . . ." Assuming that gross inconsistency may serve as a valid clue for discerning a later insertion, it is probable that the genealogy was composed by someone who believed Jesus was actually Joseph's offspring.

If the small but significant addition to the original text of Luke 1:34 is acknowledged and rejected, then the opening chapter of the Third Gospel contains two birth stories that express the Jewish outlook on dual paternity with exquisite artistry. No other chapter of the New Testament has a more Hebraic tone: even apart from the profuse allusions to and quotations from Jewish Scriptures, many idioms are Semitic.[31] The writer of the narrative doubtless had the birth story of Samuel in mind when he composed what Luke incorporated into his Gospel. Some scholars ably maintain that the birth stories were first written down in Hebrew or Aramaic and then translated into Greek.[32]

Luke's Gospel begins with the story of Elizabeth conceiving a child after the normal years of childbearing had passed. There is a marked similarity between this story of John the Baptist's birth and the story of Samson's birth.[33] In both there is an angel who announces the coming of a child to a wife who had been infertile. It is implied but not explicitly stated that the husbands Zechariah and Manoah impregnated their wives. To emphasize God's role in this divine-human triangle, the writer comments after Gabriel's visitation: "Elizabeth conceived . . . saying, 'Thus the Lord has done to me in the days when he looked on me, to take away my reproach among men.'"

The mode of conception by Elizabeth and Mary has several parallels. The announcement by Gabriel to Mary is similar in form to the announcement to Elizabeth. However, the pregnancy is less problematic for Mary, who is not considered barren. In light of the cultural patterns and languages of ancient Palestine, there is nothing unusual about the prophecy that a betrothed young woman would conceive. Betrothal in the Hebrew culture actually constituted, or by itself led to, a marital relationship.[34] Not long after the betrothal was arranged, the groom had the privilege and responsibility of having sexual relations with his bride. The Mishnah indicates that marital consummation occasionally occured while the betrothed girl was still residing in her father's house.[35]

In Judaism nonconjugal marriage was a contradiction in terms. According to the Torah it was the husband's sacred duty to give his wife her marital rights.[36] As regards this Marcus Cohn has stated: "The most important common obligation of the married couple is the performance of the marital act."[37]

In Luke's annunciation story it is unfortunate that *parthenos* has usually been translated "virgin," a word that refers to a woman who has not had sexual intercourse. The word is best defined, in both biblical and nonbiblical usage, as a girl who has reached marriageable age.[38] In Luke 1:27 *parthenos* stands in contrast to Elizabeth, who conceives in her "old age." Due to the fact that a *parthenos* was customarily married at the age of puberty, and that social sanctions protected unwed Hebrew daughters from seduction, it would have been unusual for a *parthenos* to be sexually experienced prior to betrothal. However, the word often refers to a young woman who has engaged in coitus. In the Septuagint it is used of a girl who had been raped; in classical Greek it can refer to a nonvirginal young woman; in a nonliterary papyrus the word refers to a mother; and in Jewish sepulchre inscriptions during the early Christian era it connoted someone who had married.[39]

In Luke 1:35 Gabriel informs Mary of the means by which she would conceive: "The Holy Spirit will come upon you,/ And the power of the Most High will overshadow you." In this couplet of synonymous parallelism it is discreetly stated that God will perform a husband's role. The way in which the Spirit figuratively descends upon Mary is analogous to the spread-the-husband's-skirt-over idiom for coitus in Hebrew Scriptures.[40]

It would do violence to the Hebraic outlook to interpret this bit of poetry about the Spirit's union with Mary in a literal manner. G. B. Caird perceptively comments: "It would never have occurred to a Jew to consider the overshadowing of Mary by the Holy Spirit as a substitute for normal parenthood."[41] The Hebrew religion was distinctive in the ancient world in demythologizing and thereby humanizing sexuality.[42] The God of the Hebrews was not thought of as one who actually copulated with goddesses or with human women. Consequently, Luke's account of divine paternity may well be a metaphor showing that God was active in bringing Jesus into the world. After the generation is symbolically accomplished by the Heavenly Father and biologically by the earthly husband, Mary has a gestation period and a delivery of her baby in a normal manner.

Since scholars generally agree that Luke edited written tradition pertaining to Jesus' birth which he had collected from Palestinian sources, and since there are reasons for assuming that the original story was patterned after stories of outstanding personages of Hebrew history who were conceived by the combined efforts of God, men, and women, was it Luke or some later scribe who inserted those clauses in Luke 1:34 and 3:23 that contradict the dual paternity notion?

The paucity of information about Luke makes this question a difficult one to answer. However, there are several shreds of evidence that point to someone who lived after Luke as having converted the dual paternity story into one of virginal conception. First, Luke was a disciple of Paul, who along with the rest of the apostles left no extant evidence of any belief that Jesus was virginally conceived. Second, Luke would hardly have been so inconsistent as to record that Joseph was Jesus' father in the Jerusalem Temple and in the Nazareth synagogue episodes, and state an opposing view in accounts interspersed among those early episodes of his Gospel. Third, the Greek term *epei* meaning "since," "because," etc., is used dozens of times in the New Testament, but in the writings of Luke —which amount to a third of the total New Testament literature— that common conjunction is used only to introduce the clause "since I know not a man" in Luke 1:34. In other passages Luke employed other terms to convey the same meaning, so the *epei* clause was probably inserted by someone other than Luke. Fourth, a characteristic of Luke's theology is that the Holy Spirit works through the interaction of human agents, although the process by which this occurs is not explained. For example, in Acts 13:2 the Holy Spirit mysteriously operates in the Antioch congregation, and as a consequence Paul and Barnabas are set apart for a special mission. Again, Luke tells of a vigorous discussion at a meeting of church leaders in Jerusalem, and in Acts 15:28 concludes the account with the judgment that the final consensus was the "decision of the Holy Spirit." Fifth, Luke lived in the first century of the Christian era and wrote decades before any church leaders became fascinated by Jesus' alleged virginal conception. Irenaeus is the first Christian to give clear evidence of being aware of the Matthean or Lukan nativity story,[43] so what prompted them to say that Jesus was virginally conceived was probably not first-century writings.

### THE VIRGINAL CONCEPTION DOGMA

An examination will now be made of the second-century references to Jesus' birth in order to ascertain how the theory of Jesus' virginal conception evolved. Ignatius, a bishop of Syrian Antioch in the early second century, was the first church father to write about Jesus' birth. In order to combat the Docetic denial of the full humanity of Jesus, Ignatius stressed that he was physically like other men from womb to tomb. In one letter he advises Christians to "be deaf to any talk that ignores Jesus Christ, of David's lineage, of Mary; who was really born, ate, and drank. . . ."[44] In another letter Ignatius seems to present a theory of dual paternity: "Our God, Jesus the Christ, was conceived by Mary in accordance with God's plan— being sprung both of the seed of David and from the Holy Spirit."[45] Further on in this passage, and also in another letter, Ignatius refers to mother Mary as a *parthenos.*[46] It is probable that *parthenos* here has the broader meaning of "young woman" rather than "virgin." It would have gone against Ignatius' desire to show Jesus' genuine humanity to claim that his conception was unlike that of other mortals.

An apologist named Aristides also early in the second century explained Christian belief thus: "God came down from heaven, and from a Hebrew *parthenos* assumed and clothed himself with flesh, and the Son of God lived in a daughter of man."[47] There is no indication that *parthenos* is here used to refer to a woman who conceived without human sexual relations.

Justin, who lived when the church was one century old, is the first

Christian on record to state unambiguously that Jesus was virginally conceived. Though he was aware that some Jewish Christians held Jesus to be the child of normal union between Mary and a man, Justin declared that "Christ is not man of men, begotten in the ordinary course of humanity."[48] For this he claimed to find evidence in the prophecy of Isaiah 7:14. There, according to the Septuagint, it is said that "a *parthenos* shall conceive." Justin, assuming that the text had Messianic reference and that the term *parthenos* referred to a virgin, argued with his Jewish adversary Trypho that Jesus must have been virginally conceived. In response, Trypho accurately pointed out that such a mode of birth was contrary to Jewish Messianic expectations; that Isaiah was referring to an occurrence in the immediate future; and that the terminology involved pertained to a young woman, not to a virgin.[49]

Justin's argument for a virginal conception resulted from eisegesis of Scripture, so where did such a notion originate? The question was well answered by Trypho when he pointed out that Christians were guilty of adapting pagan birth stories of demigod heroes to aid in propagandizing their religion. He said: "In Greek mythology there is a story of how Perseus was born of Danae while she was a virgin when the one whom they call Zeus descended upon her in the form of a golden shower." Then he chided: "You ought to be ashamed of reproducing this Hellenic tale and ought to admit that this Jesus is a human being of human parentage."[50] But Justin was far from being ashamed of the parallel and used it in defense of his doctrine. He asserted: "When we declare that the Logos, who is the first offspring of God, was born without sexual intercourse . . . we do not report anything different from your view about those called sons of Zeus."[51] Justin thought he was strengthening the appeal of Christianity in the Gentile world by admitting that there is really nothing unique about a virginally conceived man. Actually he was placing Christianity on a level with superstitions which many reasonable men had already discarded.

Justin, along with other postapostolic church leaders, had a strong Hellenistic background and correspondingly little understanding of the Hebraic outlook. He had studied under Greek philosophers and had adopted their moral dualism. By associating the satanic serpent with coitus, he assumed that Jesus would have been defiled by conception through a sensual union.[52] Had Justin comprehended the Hebraic concept of dual paternity he would not have glibly presupposed that physical passion and spiritual power could not coexist in a person.

Tertullian, writing around A.D. 200, followed Justin's line of defense by making an analogy to Hellenistic legends of miraculous conceptions. The manner of Jesus' birth was described by that prominent Latin church father thus:

The Son of God has a mother touched by no impurity. . . . When a ray is projected from the sun, it is a portion of the whole; but the sun will be in the ray. . . . The source of the substance remains whole and undiminished even if you borrow many offshoots of its quality from it. Thus what has proceeded from God, is God and God's Son and both are one. . . . This ray of God . . . entered into a certain virgin, and, in her womb fashioned into flesh, is born, man mingled with God.[53]

Tertullian acknowledged that his treatment of Jesus' virginal conception was like some pagan stories of unnatural liaisons. The parallel he may have had in mind is the myth of the sun god Apollo siring Alexander the Great. A divine ray penetrated his mother, and this, rather than intercourse with Philip, allegedly caused her pregnancy. Plutarch says of that conception: "The night before the marriage was consummated, the bride dreamed that there was a clap of thunder, that a bolt fell upon her womb, and that from the stroke a great fire was kindled, which broke into flames that went out in all directions and then was extinguished."[54]

In the folklore of the ancient Mediterranean world there was wide circulation of stories attributing to teachers and kings a divine paternity in the absence of human male procreators.[55] Such stories were told of Buddha,[56] Pythagoras,[57] Plato,[58] Augustus,[59] and Apollonius.[60]

In the latter half of the second century, when the canon of the New Testament was becoming established, it is probable that some scribe modified the Lukan and Matthean accounts in order to give Jesus a beginning as spectacular as that of prominent figures in the Greco-Roman world. Whoever did it no doubt believed he was doing a service to Christianity by removing holy Jesus from the Greek idea of defilement he thought would ensue had Jesus been

generated on a bed soiled by erotic passion. Around A.D. 200 a
Christian gave this explanation: "Our Lord Jesus Christ was born of
a virgin only for the following reason: he was to bring to naught the
begetting that proceeds from lawless appetite, and show the ruler of
this world that God could form man even without human sexual
intercourse."[61] Here is stated the anti-Hebraic outlook that sexual
desire and its fulfillment are contrary to the law of God and that
those who are immaculately pure must renounce it completely.

With respect to the church's distortion of the Hebraic view of
sexuality expressed in the opening story of Luke's Gospel, Thomas
Walker's judgment has much to commend it. In his book *Is Not This
the Son of Joseph?* he wrote:

The original beauty of the early document, which was here utilized by the
evangelist, has been spoiled by someone, whose mind was as far removed
as possible from the mind of the composer of the document. . . . The Virgin
Birth idea was an error of the Greek-minded leaders of the early Church
in the second century, who . . . never really got entirely free from the
erroneous notion of their upbringing, that the human body was the seat of
evil. . . . They lamentably misinterpreted a Semitic story of the conception
of a child of Hebrew parents.[62]

After the second-century orthodox doctrine had crystallized, and
the idea of Jesus' virgin conception was incorporated in basic dogma,
the theory of dual paternity was lost. Its last trace in the early church
is found in the *Gospel of Philip* which was discovered in Egypt in
1945. The authors of that noncanonical gospel assert that they were
"Hebrews" prior to becoming Christians.[63] They present the traditional Hebraic outlook in declaring that Jesus was both the offspring
of Joseph the carpenter and the child of the Heavenly Father who
"united with the virgin."[64] They also made this rather strained
deduction: "The Lord would not have said 'My Father in heaven'
unless he had another father; he would have simply said 'My Father.' "[65]

The pillars of orthodoxy in the patristic era twisted the earliest
Christian testimony by claiming that Jesus was discontinuous with
humanity since his mother's womb was not fertilized by the sperm
of a male. By treating Mary's conception as an unnatural occurrence
they magnified out of proportion the significance of the nativity in

the life of Jesus and in the life of nascent Christianity. In the New Testament the circumstances of Jesus' birth are peripheral: no comment is recorded of Jesus or his apostles concerning a miraculous conception. Yet in the creeds of the church the mode of Jesus' birth usually has as significant a place as his sufferings and resurrection. Indeed the Nicene Creed, that most important creed of the fourth century, implies that there is nothing worth affirming about Jesus' earthly life except his virginal birth and his manner of death. In the New Testament the uniqueness of Jesus was bound up with his life-style, which incarnated love, justice, and freedom, but in orthodoxy there has been emphasis upon his being born in a manner removed from so-called tainted sensual pleasure and the corrupted sperm of Adam. The eminent theologian Athanasius articulated the settled outlook of the fourth century church when he stated that the Logos took a human body "directly from a spotless, stainless virgin, without the agency of human father—a pure body, untainted by intercourse with man."[66] In all major branches of the Eastern and Western church, the Athanasian position has been regarded as an infallible truth, and therefore it has only infrequently been questioned. Reformed theologian Karl Barth has given the doctrine its most sophisticated defense. He declares that "the sinful life of sex is excluded as the source of the human existence of Jesus Christ. . . . The event of sex cannot be considered at all as the sign of the divine *agape* which seeks not its own and never fails. . . . If Christ were the son of a male He would be a sinner like all the rest."[67]

### EARTHLY AND HEAVENLY FATHERS

Some scientific objections to Christianity are dissolved if the biblical view of God's presence at human conception is used to interpret the nativity stories of the canonical Gospels. Most persons who comprehend modern biology do not have the credulity to believe that a virginal conception literally could or did happen. They realize that parthenogenesis for a male human being is probably a genetic impossibility. Ancient though it is, the dual paternity theory also dispenses with the idea of nonphysical insemination, so it is not at fisticuffs with modern thought. That theory also dissipates another biological difficulty in the orthodox view. From Augustine onward it has been believed that sexual desire is inherently sinful and that it is naturally inherited, like skin pigmentation.[68] Moreover, the church accepted the prevailing Greek view of reproduction and thought that the sperm contained the full human character, with the female merely providing the receptacle for nourishing the male's preformed baby. Hence it was believed that a virginally conceived Jesus could not inherit sin, for a mother could not transmit human qualities to her child. However, in the nineteenth century, the female ovum was discovered and it is now recognized that both male and female contribute equally to the genetic characteristics of their offspring. Thus the orthodox doctrine which maintains that Jesus was congenitally undefiled because Mary was isolated from sperm infected by Adam is bankrupt. It was a blunder ever to attempt to build the idea of the perfection of Jesus on genetic foundations. The New Testament writers held that Jesus was without sin because of his godly decisions and actions throughout his ministry.

The revival of the theory of dual paternity would result in a fuller recognition that divine intervention does not exclude human cooperation. This should be corrective to the supernaturalists who find the divine mainly in events in which "sense is dumb and flesh retires." Those who can find nothing spiritual in carnal entwining need to recall that the first blessing in the Bible is on marital sexuality. The frowning disapproval of sexual passion in the history of Western civilization has been influenced in no little degree by those who have wrongly given an asexual interpretation to the relationship between Mary and Joseph and then have exalted them as the models of holiness.

Conversely, the secular naturalist should see in a theory of dual paternity that human endeavors do not exclude the divine presence. The God of the Bible is found more in the warp and woof of ordinary human life than in inexplicable extraordinary events. Human sexuality can be not only a means of hedonistic gratification but also an area where God's love and mercy are discerned. So this theory may provide a middle ground which is more adequate than polar positions all too often evoked by consideration of Jesus' nativity. Those who champion the dual paternity theory see the conception of Jesus not as a case of *either* the Spirit giving life to Mary's ovum *or* Joseph's sperm fertilizing it. Rather Jesus was *both* the pure incarnation of God *and* a complete human being formed through the union of male and female genes.

J. A. T. Robinson has pointed out that the purpose of the story of Mary conceiving Jesus by divine intervention was to make a positive claim about the Spirit, not a negative assertion about the flesh. He rightly interprets the story as being on as different a level from the science of genetics as Genesis is from geology. It is saying, he claims, "that the significance of Jesus is not to be comprehended *simply* at the level of heredity and environment."[69]

In conclusion an adaptation of Darwin's postscript to his *Descent of Man* is in order.

I am aware that the conclusions arrived at in this work will be denounced by some as highly irreligious; but he who denounces them is bound to show why it is more irreligious to explain the conception of Jesus through the laws of ordinary reproduction than to explain the origin of man as a distinct species by descent from some lower form, through the laws of variation and natural selection. The birth of individuals and species are equally parts of that grand sequence of events which our minds refuse to accept as the result of blind chance.[70]

## 2

# The Maturing of Rabbi Jesus

UNDERSTANDING a person's sexuality involves probing his environmental as well as his hereditary background. Since we have examined in the previous chapter Jesus' genetic inheritance, attention will now be given to integrating facets of his postnatal sexuality with the rest of his acculturation.

Judging from Western art, Christians do not often picture Jesus as an ancient Palestinian Jew. This is true of the early representations as well as of the blond, blue-eyed portraits found in modern art. The early paintings of Jesus, dating more than two centuries after his death, usually depict a haloed figure in a white toga. Such an image would have been more appropriate for a Gentile teacher such as Pythagoras. Before the Christian era, "in Greek and Roman art the heads of gods, heroes, and distinguished citizens were often portrayed with a circle of light or a rayed fillet about the head."[1] More particularly, an ancient biographer of Pythagoras informs us that "his robe was white and spotless."[2]

Artists give little attention to the feature of Jesus' clothing that identified him as a Jew. Every devout Jew wore a distinctive fringe on his clothing as prescribed by the Torah.[3] Yet few paintings of Jesus show the tassels attached to the edges of his outer garment to which references are made in the Gospels.[4]

The perennial distortions of Jesus' probable external appearance are symptomatic of a more serious malady. Culturally conditioned mental images of Jesus have been projected onto the screen of the Christian's imagination. In the medieval era he was thought of as an ascetic monk; men of the Age of Enlightenment viewed him as a rationalist; others have conceived of him as an idealized Rousseauan romanticist, Marxian socialist, or Kierkegaardian existentialist.

Recognizing human foibles, it may be unavoidable that our internal creations of a historical model of morality display little more than a clustering of the admirable characteristics of a current hero. But the one-sided representation of Jesus in every century since his death has also been due to a lack of genuine information about his social environment which is no longer unavoidable. The church fathers, who lived after the destruction of the Jewish state and before the fall of Rome, had few opportunities to talk with Jewish scholars or Palestinian natives. With one or two notable exceptions, the church fathers could not even read Hebrew. Later, in medieval times, it was a rare scholastic who had access to rabbinic literature even if he desired to learn of the ancient Jewish culture.

Some modern literary attempts to picture Jesus as a Gentile Christian rather than as a Palestinian Jew seem to be a deliberate effort to be invidious. Since one device for making a portrait literally outstanding is to set a luminous face in bold relief, Jesus has been exalted by darkening his Jewish background. A notable example of this approach is found in the influential writings of Alfred Edersheim, a Jew of the past century who became a convert to Christianity. He engaged in a vast investigation of Jewish tradition for the purpose of showing "the infinite distance between Christ and the teaching of the synagogue."[5] Edersheim's voluminous *Life and Times of Jesus the Messiah* is devoted to proving that the substance and spirit of Jesus' teaching was absolutely contrary to Judaism, even though it was cast in Jewish form.[6] To expose the absurdity of this evaluation, at least on one basic point, one need do no more than realize that Akiba, a leading rabbi in the century when Jesus lived, pointed to "Love your neighbor as yourself" as the comprehensive law of the Torah.[7]

Edersheim's point of view may be expressed by this figure: God ripped out Jesus by a Caesarean operation from a dying Judaism. When Christians who share this outlook write about the postexilic period of Jewish history, they imply that earlier religious vitality was exhausted and that little was left at the beginning of the Christian era beyond a calcified casuistry. Yet during that period many Psalms were written which profoundly influenced Jesus. This was also the time when the synagogue became established as the hub of Jewish life. A perusal of the *Mishnah*, the rabbinic record of the era in which

Jesus lived, displays that delight in studying the Torah—not lethargic ritualism—was the pervading spirit of that sector of Palestinian Judaism which had the greatest impact on Jesus.

In view of the ready availability nowadays of a variety of extra-biblical writings by participants in the ancient Palestinian culture, coupled with a heightened awareness of the importance of cultural milieu in understanding an individual, there is now no more excuse for fanciful projections onto the figure of Jesus of later conceptions of ideal life-styles. The findings of archaeologists in this century together with the results of textual and historical criticism of ancient documents put serious students today in a better position to know accurately about the era in which Jesus lived than scholars in any other century since his death.

The first step in comprehending the historical Jesus is the full realization that he was raised by faithful Jews and that his Jewishness persisted throughout life in spite of his rigorous criticism of conventional Judaism. Accordingly, in the discussion that follows the Gospel testimony will be dovetailed with comments pertaining to the training of youth culled from ancient Jewish sources. After gaining a more adequate understanding of Jesus' formative years, an attempt will be made to ascertain the degree to which he became independent of his acculturation.

## FROM CIRCUMCISION TO MARRIAGE

G. F. Moore, in his definitive *Judaism in the First Centuries of the Christian Era,* has pointed out that early Judaism singled out five principal responsibilities of a father to his son.[8] The duties are recorded in the *Talmud* in this sequential way: "He must circumcise him, redeem him, teach him Torah, teach him a trade, and find him a wife."[9]

Circumcision, the first duty, had a sexual as well as a cultic purpose. It originated as a puberty rite and was associated with making a young man fit for marriage.[10] Philo explains that it was performed for the physical purpose of facilitating sexual intercourse.[11] Early in Hebrew history infant circumcision was substituted for the more severe operation which had been performed when a boy came of age.

For the Hebrews the religious significance of circumcision was paramount. It was the mark of belonging to God's convenantal community.[12] Rabbi Akiba held that circumcision symbolized the consecration to God of the physical body.[13] But why was the penis singled out for special honor? Apropos of this question Martin Buber has written: "Sex is hallowed by the sacrament of the circumcision covenant which survives in its original purity and not only confirms the act of begetting but converts it into a holy vocation."[14] A fuller answer is given by sociologist David Mace:

Every Hebrew man carried on his body the mark of his identity as a member of God's chosen race. And it was no accident that he carried this mark on his sex organ. Far from being disreputable, this was the most sacred part of his whole body; therefore it was appropriate that it should be specially dedicated to God as the symbol that his whole body, his whole person, was dedicated to God. For it was with this organ that he became, in a special sense, a co-worker with God.[15]

Joshua, the baby whom the Greek writers of the New Testament called Jesus, was circumcised and shortly thereafter dedicated to the Lord at the Temple. At the latter ceremony, in accordance with Mosaic law, an animal sacrifice was presented to "redeem" the first-born son in remembrance of God's liberation of the Israelites from Egypt.[16] This scrupulous observance by Jesus' parents of what righteous Jews were expected to do is one of several indications that they should not be classified by the technical term *amme-ha-aretz* (people of the land). Herbert Danby has accurately defined this phrase as pertaining to Jews who were ignorant of the Torah and who failed to observe regulations regarding purification.[17]

Luke also shows that Jesus' parents went beyond the traditional requirements. The Mishnah states that Jewish men were expected to visit the Temple occasionally.[18] But according to Luke 2:41, both parents devoted a number of days each year to traveling the considerable distance from Nazareth to Jerusalem to attend the Passover feast.

Of all parental duties, teaching children about the Jewish religious heritage was given first priority. Josephus speaks for fellow Jews when he writes: "Our principal concern is to educate our children and we think it to be the most important business of our whole life."[19] In the Shema, the Jewish affirmation of faith, fathers obligated themselves to communicate the Mosaic commandments to their sons in the process of day-to-day living.[20] Jesus began to learn the basic theology of his culture from Joseph and Mary at the earliest possible stage in his development. Philo, writing during Jesus' lifetime, informs us that Jews "from their very swaddling clothes are taught by parents, teachers, and those who bring them up, even before instruction in the sacred laws and unwritten customs, to believe in one God, the Father and Creator of the world."[21]

The focus on God as father would have been especially meaningful to a child. That metaphor was taken from Jewish Scriptures and was frequently used in the era when Jesus lived.[22] Even the Aramaic diminutive for father, *abba,* was employed by Jewish leader Choni in referring to God.[23] It is significant that one of the first words in Jesus' vocabulary—*abba,* daddy—was sanctioned for use in speaking both to his human father and to his heavenly Father. Two petitions which children prayed daily were: "Cause us to turn, O our Father, to Thy law," and "Forgive us, our Father, for we have sinned."[24] In accord with this filial mode of speaking, a faithful Jew considered himself a son of God.[25]

As regards formal schooling the *Mishnah* states: "At five years old one is fit for the Scripture, at ten for the Mishnah, at thirteen for the fulfilling of the commandments, at fifteen for the Talmud. . . ."[26] During the era in which Jesus lived there had probably been established in local communities an elementary school called the House of the Book *(Bet-ha-Sefer).*[27] It was appropriately named, since the Torah was its sole textbook. The school was conducted by the synagogue superintendent *(hazzan),* who instructed boys in reading and writing by means of recitations from the Hebrew Torah. The intermediate school, named the House of Study *(Bet-ha-Midrash)*[28] was also administered by the community synagogue. Popular instruction was given in the oral tradition as well as in the written Scriptures.[29] This school was conducted on Sabbath afternoons, so that those who participated in this study could also engage in daily work.

It is probable that Jesus attended both of the above schools before puberty. Then, around the age of thirteen, he "fulfilled the commandments" and acquired the status of an adult[30]—an occasion medieval Judaism would call Bar-Mitzvah. At that time he was expected to have an adequate knowledge of his culture's spiritual and social heritage. Josephus, for instance, claimed that he had acquired an accurate knowledge of the Torah by the age of fourteen.[31] He asserted that a Jewish child had had the laws of his culture so engraved on him that he could recall them even more readily than his own name![32]

The only Gospel writer who provides any information about Jesus' boyhood is Luke. This has suggested to some critics that he was troubled by the earliest Gospel's having no treatment of Jesus' life prior to his public ministry and accordingly filled in the biographical void by a fictitious story. But in the prologue to his Gospel Luke displays the marks of a serious historian, for he there gives value to accuracy and firsthand observation. Robert Grant cogently demonstrates that Luke's methodology is similar to that of ancient Greek historians such as Aelius Theon.[33] From the evidence Grant presents, for critical evaluation of sources by ancient historians, it may be concluded that those who suppose that concern for factual accuracy in describing the founder of Christianity has arisen only in recent centuries show little more than a prejudice against ancient scholarship. Although the "many" whom Luke acknowledged as having undertaken to compile a narrative of the Jesus movement before him may well have recorded some legendary accretions, it was Luke's stated purpose to provide authentic knowledge about the beginnings of Christianity. The burden of the proof rests on those who claim that Luke's record of the early years of Jesus' life is essentially unreliable.

Luke gives a graphic description of the maturing Jesus. On his visit to the traditional capital of his country at the age of twelve, he sought out some Jerusalem teachers in order to learn about current theological issues. Jesus joined these men, showing the traits of a serious student—that is, combining active inquiry with absorbing what the Torah authorities had to say. He "sat among the teachers, listening to them and asking them questions."[34] The question-and-answer method was common to Jewish instruction.[35] Thus the well-known paintings of this scene which show Jesus preaching to the rabbis distort what Luke was trying to convey. The teachers were amazed at Jesus' understanding—not because he presumed to be their instructor. Jesus' role is described in this advice to another student by a pre-Christian Jewish teacher: "When you stand among your elders, decide who is wise and join him. Listen gladly to every godly argument and see that no wise proverb escapes you."[36]

It is possible that Hillel and/or Shammai, the most prominent Jewish debaters at the time of Jesus' birth, were still alive and teaching in Jerusalem, and Jesus may have been introduced to the liberal interpretation of the Torah championed by Hillel and his disciples. Two principles of Hillel seem to have had special impact upon him. One was: "Judge not your neighbor until you put yourself in his place."[37] The other teaching is contained in a story of someone who came to Shammai and Hillel requesting to be taught the whole Torah during the time that he could stand on one leg. He first went to Shammai who drove him away. Hillel, however, endorsed Tobit's maxim, "What you hate do not do to anyone," and commented, "That is the entire law; all the rest is commentary."[38]

Did Jesus' education extend beyond the age of puberty, when he would have attained adult status? It has usually been assumed that his educational opportunities were limited to the rudimentary instruction provided for all Jewish boys. Those maintaining this position accept the outlook of Jesus' adversaries as represented by the Fourth Gospel, where some Jews wonder, "How is it that this untrained man has such learning?"[39] Becoming well-informed is not dependent upon formal education, so it is plausible that Jesus' remarkable knowledge was acquired independently of his schooling. On the other hand, higher education was available in ancient Judaism[40] and he may have participated in it. This would harmonize with Rabbi Klausner's claim regarding Jesus: "He is as expert in the Scriptures as the best of the Pharisees, and he is quite at home with the Pharisee's expository devices. He is saturated with the great ideas of the Prophets and the Psalms."[41] More recently David Flusser, a New Testament specialist at Hebrew University in Jerusalem, has maintained that Jesus had the finest Jewish education available: "He was perfectly at home both in holy scripture, and in oral tradition, and knew how to apply his scholarly heritage."[42]

Concomitant with Torah study was training in a craft. It was incumbent upon all fathers to provide vocational instruction for their male offspring, for, as a Jewish saying put it, "He who does not teach his son a trade, teaches him to steal."[43] Another saying points to the moral necessity of balancing religious pursuits with physically demanding work: "It is excellent to combine study of the Torah with a secular occupation, for toil in them both puts sin out of mind."[44] Thus Hillel combined inquiry into his religious heritage with the work of a common laborer,[45] and Paul became knowledgeable in both Judaism and tentmaking.[46] In a parallel manner it is likely that Jesus became skilled at interpreting Scripture during the period of his life when he was apprenticed to his carpenter father.[47] Even those whose primary calling was interpreting the Jewish religious tradition were expected to gain their livelihood in ways other than charging for their instruction. Hillel warned against teaching for compensation: "He that makes a profit off the Torah removes his life from the world."[48]

The last of the five duties laid down for a Jewish father was that of arranging a marriage for his son. In the patriarchal society in which Jesus lived, a young man was generally given little voice in deciding who his wife would be. Around the time when a son was physically mature his father made a betrothal agreement with the guardian of an eligible girl.[49] To delay this more than a decade beyond puberty was forbidden, and there is no definite indication of violators in any of the sects of ancient Judaism.[50] Hillel and Shammai, though differing on many points of scriptural interpretation, were united in affirming that no righteous man can abstain from keeping God's first command, "Be fruitful and multiply."[51] But the procreation of legitimate offspring was only one reason why the Jews considered marriage to be a necessity. The responsibilities of marital life were considered a testing ground for developing sturdy character. In this regard Rabbi Claude Montefiore has stated: "Judaism has consistently deprecated and depreciated celibacy; it has required its saints to show their sanctity in the world amid the ties and obligations of family life."[52] Not least, marriage was obligatory because Judaism regarded sexual pleasure as a gift of God which should not be soiled by illicit indulgence.[53]

It is probable that Jesus married as a young man, even though there is no more mention in the New Testament of his fulfillment of that requirement than there is of his attending school in Nazareth. According to Semitic tradition it was as obligatory for a father to find a wife for his son as to teach him and circumcise him. Hence, even if there were no reference in the Gospels to Jesus' circumcision, it would be wrong to conclude that his father neglected or rejected that duty. Just as the *Koran* does not mention circumcision and takes the obligation of marriage for granted, so the Gospels do not mention the circumcision or marriage of most of the men who are discussed in it. This is due to the fact that those social institutions were practiced in a thoroughgoing manner in the Semitic culture. Deviations from normative behavior are more likely to be remembered and thus lodged in oral and written traditions, so it makes sense to assume that Jesus and his apostles were all circumcised and married.

After a Jewish man became adept at Torah interpretation, skilled at a craft, and successfully married, he was, according to the *Sayings of the Fathers,* "fit at thirty for authority." If he desired to instruct others the last qualification was stressed. A Mishnaic injunction states categorically: "An unmarried man may not be a teacher."[54] In a recent study, Schalom Ben-Chorin of Jerusalem argues that Jesus married because an unmarried teacher was unimaginable in the culture in which he participated. We know nothing about the wives of Hillel, Shammai, Jesus, and many other notable men of that era and culture, Ben-Chorin admits, but had they been unmarried, surely their opponents would have pointed to their violation of sacred duty as a basis for criticism.[55]

## THE IMPACT OF RABBINIC MORALITY

Intrinsic to assessing the sexuality of Jesus during the last years of his life is ascertaining the degree to which he internalized the sexual standards of the respected religious leaders of his own culture. While most Christians are willing to grant that Jesus was raised in a pious family of the Jewish community, they assume that he completely broke away from his societal norms as he attained maturity. For example, the Vatican official journal has declared that it is fallacious to relate to Jesus the prevailing outlook on sexuality of the ancient Jewish community because "Christ was anything but conditioned by the cultural and religious atmosphere of his time."[56]

I shall attempt to demonstrate that this position on Jesus' sexuality, which has been articulated in Catholicism recently and is echoed in other churches, is no more than a half-truth. Some close parallels between the values and actions of Jesus and the leaders of rabbinic Judaism will be noted, as well as some major ways in which he set his course against traditional mores.

Luke informs his readers that Jesus "was about thirty years of age" when he began his ministry. At that time Jesus taught in the Galilean synagogues and was regarded by Jews as a religious authority.[57] The fact that he was asked for scriptural interpretations shows that he was acknowledged as having scholarly competence. In the Gospels he is presented as one who quotes or alludes to many books of Hebrew Scripture. During Jesus' lifetime a new designation, "Rabbi" or "Rabboni," was emerging as a title for men with such gifts. Hillel and Shammai were not so called a generation earlier, but from the first century of the Christian era onward the term came to supersede all others as a designation for a teacher of Judaism.

Even though Christians rarely if ever refer to the founder of their religion as *Rabbi* Jesus, the title is, as Günther Bornkamm and W. D. Davies point out, one of the more adequte ways of designating his historical role.[58] While extremely skeptical of using the New Testament as a source of biographical information about Jesus, Rudolf Bultmann admits: "If the Gospel record is worthy of credence, it is at least clear that Jesus actually lived as a Jewish rabbi."[59] There are more than a dozen instances in the Gospels of Jesus' friends and adversaries addressing him as Rabbi. He was thought of as a rabbi more often than is apparent from the Greek Gospels or their English translations. Luke translates the Hebrew title used by Mark either as Lord *(kurios)* or Master *(epistates)* for the benefit of his Gentile readers.[60] Also, in each of the Gospels Jesus is addressed by the Greek term for teacher *(didaskalos)*, even though he was not so called by his fellow Jews, who spoke Aramaic or Hebrew. It would be anachronistic to assume that the appellation *Rabbi* implied some kind of official ordination at that time.[61] But it does show the spontaneous respect given to one who was an expert in the theology of Judaism and exemplary in its practice. Indeed, the honor of being entitled Rabbi was such that Jesus warned his disciples of the haughtiness that could easily corrupt persons so designated.[62]

The similarity between the teaching of Rabbi Jesus and his Jewish peers is illustrated by mutual denunciations of hypocrisy. Jesus frequently exposed the self-righteous, blind to the gap between what they pretended to be and what they practiced. In a work probably written by a Palestinian contemporary of Jesus, the sham piety of some fellow Jews is likewise castigated: "Their hands and their minds are unclean and their mouths are full of boasting. Yet they say: 'Do not touch me lest you pollute me.' "[63] Another pseudepigraphal writing of the same general place and period contains this curse: "Let God remove those that live in hypocrisy in the company of the pious. . . . Let ravens peck out the eyes of the hypocrites."[64] It is unfortunate that Pharisaism is now regarded as a synonym for hypocrisy, for that vice was condemned as severely by the ancient Pharisees as by Jesus.[65] In their literature they list seven types of Pharisees, most of whom are disapproved of because they fall short of what Pharisees profess to be.[66]

Another way in which Jesus was like some fellow rabbis was in gaining a reputation as a healer. Much of the attention Jesus was accorded in the villages he visited was due to his faith healing activity. The cures he was able to accomplish with the cooperation of those afflicted ranged from removal of a skin disease (improperly called "leprosy") to the revival of those presumed dead. A Galilean contemporary of Jesus, Rabbi Hanina ben Dosa, was also famous for his gift of restoring sick people to health.[67] Moreover, the Talmud attributes marvelous healings to Rabbi Jochanan ben Zakkai and to Rabbi Eliezer ben Hyrcanus, who lived at the same time.[68] An ancient scriptural commentary even claims that at least one rabbi had the power to resuscitate the dead.[69] Jesus defended his efforts to heal those presumed to be demon-possessed by acknowledging that his exorcisms were similar to those of other Jews.[70]

It is difficult for Christians who know of Jesus' culture only through the incomplete New Testament descriptions of it to accept without reservation that Jesus was throughout life a Jew—not to mention a Jewish rabbi. Although all his disciples during his lifetime were Jews, in the Fourth Gospel "the Jews" is used without qualification dozens of times to refer to the enemies of Jesus. That unfair generalization has prompted some to assume that he completely cast aside Judaism during his public ministry. However, Jesus not only had a high regard for his countrymen to the end of his life, but viewed the Pharisees—the party of the rabbis and scribes—as the people with the most adequate understanding of God's will. That evaluation by Jesus is expressed in several places in the Gospels. When a scribe affirmed that the commandments to love God and one's neighbor were more important than ceremonial offerings, Jesus responded, "You are not far from the kingdom of God."[71] Even in a collection of taunts against the scribes and Pharisees, Jesus advised his disciples to accept their teachings but be wary of the way they act on their own principles.[72] Annulling the Pharisaic interpretations of the Torah was not so much Jesus' aim as to go beyond them to something more complete. Thus righteousness should exceed that of the scribes and Pharisees. For example, Jesus regarded their tithing favorably, but faulted them for being overly scrupulous in that practice at the expense of neglecting justice and the love of God.[73]

Although a cursory reading of the Gospels seems to show Jesus in fundamental opposition to the Pharisees, it is more accurate to say that Jesus was participating in a vigorous rabbinic debate. The saying, "When two rabbis argue there will be three opinions," has been characteristic of Judaism throughout its long history. The Sabbath law debate, frequently treated in the New Testament and in the Mishnah, shows that Rabbi Jesus was advocating a position not basically different from some others in the mainstream of Judaism. In his time no authoritative position had been established on how the Sabbath should be observed. Hillel and Shammai, as well as other scribes, argued over the most satisfactory way of putting into practice the Decalogue command to keep the Sabbath holy. In general Jesus supported the more liberal position articulated by Hillel.[74] His teaching that "the Sabbath was made for man" corresponds to a general principle expressed in a source of ancient Judaism: "The Sabbath is given over to you, not you to the Sabbath."[75] Rabbi Klausner along with other Jewish and Christian authorities agrees that Jesus' basic outlook on Sabbath law "is quite in accordance with the Pharisaic point of view."[76] Both Jesus and the moderate Pharisees realized that the Mosaic statement of the Sabbath law had both humanitarian and theological purposes—to afford relaxation from daily labor and to provide an opportunity for divine worship.

The Pharisees detailed thirty-nine types of ordinary work prohibited on the Sabbath, but with this important qualification: "Whenever there is doubt as to whether a life may be in danger, the laws

of the Sabbath may be suspended."[77] Jesus emphasized even more
strongly the factor of human need and argued that treatment of
illness on the Sabbath should not be limited to extreme cases. He
aimed not to destroy the Sabbath law but to revitalize it by reducing
the legal restrictions advocated by some. He would have sympathized with this witty Mishnaic observation: "The rules about the
Sabbath . . . are as mountains hanging by a hair, for Scripture is
scanty and the rules many."[78]

In defending his rejection of some of the then current Sabbath law
casuistry, Jesus appealed to Scriptures like a skilled rabbi. He maintained that the prevailing view that all Sabbath reaping of grain is
forbidden is inconsistent with an episode in David's life; when he
and his men were hungry they set aside ritual law to accommodate
human need.[79] Jesus also quoted Hosea's understanding of God, "I
desire mercy, not sacrifice," to reinforce this contention.[80] It is seen
then that Jesus did not slavishly follow past interpretations as a
mediocre scribe might do. It is understandable that Galilean syna-
gogue-goers "were astonished at his teaching, for he taught them as
one who had authority, and not as the scribes."[81] His study of
Scripture gave him a profound awareness of the will of God for
human culture and he spoke about it with freedom.

It would be unbalanced to present only ways in which Jesus and
some Pharisees shared similar outlooks regarding hypocrisy, healing, and observing the Sabbath. Jesus differed from the Pharisees in
one fundamental way—in his attitude toward those who did not
measure up to the Pharisees' standard of conduct.[82] The Pharisees
believed in salvation through segregation from those who had neither the inclination nor the leisure to abide strictly by the sacred
Jewish customs. The party name Pharisee (perhaps from *perushim*,
"set apart") was probably derived from the Pharisees' conviction
that they should keep themselves from defiling contacts.[83] According to the Fourth Gospel the Pharisees sneered; "This crowd, who
do not know the law, are accursed."[84] That contemptuous attitude
corresponded to what one of the more gentle scribes said about
those *amme-ha-aretz*. Hillel declared: "An *am-ha-aretz* cannot be religious."[85] It was forbidden for a righteous Jew to visit or trade with
such a person.[86] Even the touch of the garment of an *am-ha-aretz* was
defiling.[87] The Mosaic law, "Cursed be the man who lies with any

beast," was applied to the marriage of a scribe with a woman from the rank of the *amme-ha-aretz,* "for they are loathsome and their women are unclean vermin."[88]

Jesus found the snobbish aloofness of the Palestinian religious establishment appalling and thought that Pharisees should come out from their holy huddles and be compassionate toward those who did not meet the purification requirements of Judaism. In his belief that moral defilement does not come from external associations,[89] Jesus shunned no one. Befriending lepers, beggars, and tax-collectors, he rejected the idea that God saved those who avoided contact with the disreputable. When criticized for dining with the *amme-ha-aretz,* whom the Pharisees called "sinners," Jesus retorted, "Those who are well have no need of a physician, but those who are sick: I came not to call the righteous, but sinners."[90] He introduced the radical principle of salvation through companionship with the morally sick, and turned into a human endeavor what Ezekiel had claimed was God's activity: "I will seek the lost, and I will bring back the strayed, and I will bind up the crippled, and I will strengthen the weak."[91] Apropos of this Rabbi Montefiore has rightly commented: "The rabbis attached no less value to repentence than Jesus. . . . But to *seek out* the sinner, and instead of avoiding the bad companion, to choose him as your friend in order to work his moral redemption, this was, I fancy, something new in the religious history of Israel."[92] The way Jesus conducted himself would later be stated philosophically as Kant's famous imperative. He believed that every person should be treated as a dignified end in himself and never as a means only.

### JESUS INDEPENDENCE OF JUDAISM

In a self-descriptive way Jesus remarked: "Every scribe who has been trained for the kingdom of heaven is like a householder who brings out of his treasure what is new and what is old."[93] He was a scriptural scholar who depended upon the religious leaders of Israel and upon rabbinic Judaism for many of his gems of insight. Like all creative geniuses he borrowed and assimilated whatever he could find of value among the competing authorities of his day, and disregarded the trivial. Having a temperament of exceptional receptiveness to what was vital in religion, he was able to discern the pattern of divine providence as it was interpreted over the centuries by spokesmen of the Lord. He mastered the best of the past as he grew to maturity and then was able to sprint far beyond it. There is an originality in Jesus' teaching and a life-style that transcends his predecessors. But his unique vision of the nature of true religion was possible because he stood on the shoulders of Israel's prophets, psalmists, and scribes.

Some of the autobiographical testimony of the apostle Paul might well be applied to Jesus: "Circumcised on the eighth day, of the people of Israel, . . . a Hebrew of the Hebrews." "I advanced in Judaism beyond many of my own age among my people in my intense devotion to the traditions of my forefathers."[94] Both Jesus and Paul were born and bred in the culture of rabbinic Judaism. Both may have been Pharisees, although the New Testament explicitly states only that Paul belonged to that Jewish sect. That neither was from the *amme-ha-aretz* may be inferred from the information Paul gives about himself and from the fact that Pharisees discussed the Torah with Jesus and even invited him to dinner. Jesus' dress also gives evidence of his standing in the learned community. Rabbi Ben Azzai disclosed an ancient custom in commenting that a scribe can be distinguished from an *am-ha-aretz* by the fact that the latter does not wear tassels on his garment.[95]

When both "grew in favor with God" they rejected some of the teachings of traditional Judaism. Thus Jesus had compassion for the *amme-ha-aretz* and others generally disdained by Judaism. Had he been a member of that low class, there would have been nothing unusual in his special consideration for his fellow outcasts and hence probably nothing remembered of his kindness toward them in the traditions that became recorded as the Gospels.

The mature Jesus referred to his teachings and way of life as "new wine" that must be placed in fresh wineskins.[96] In this analogy Jesus was asserting that some of his commitments could not fit into the outworn forms of a bygone age. But that declaration of independence from Judaism should be interpreted in the way Thomas Jefferson viewed the freedom movement of the American colonists against Britain. The drafter of the Declaration of Independence would have been the first to admit his profound and abiding indebtedness throughout his life to the English common law tradition and to the democratic polity of John Locke. It is probable that Jesus likewise thought of himself not so much as a champion of novel ideas as a conserver of the quintessence of his heritage. In order to clear the Anglo-American political stream of some royal obstructions that were hindering the flow of liberty, Jefferson composed a piece of propaganda which served as the dynamite needed to permit it to run more freely. Jesus also indulged in hyperbolic criticism of the Judaism of his day so that the good news prophesied by Isaiah could "set at liberty those who are oppressed."[97] He saw himself as a participant in the main currents of a covenantal community which stretched back to Father Abraham and was ever moving toward a society "whose builder and maker is God." That "householder" blended together old and new treasures and discarded what could not be integrated into the total ecumenical plan.

# 3

## *Jesus the Philogynist*

ONE of the most extraordinary but least acknowledged ways in which Jesus differed from his culture was in his relationship with women. In a recent scholarly study of Palestine at the beginning of Christianity, Joachim Jeremias points out that a male teacher attracting women disciples was "an unprecedented happening in the history of that time."[1] It was then customary for only young men to follow after a charismatic leader. The position of the women who followed him was no more demeaning than that of their leader, for Luke uses the same verb *diakonein* ("to wait on") to refer to the ministry of both Jesus and the women with him.[2] Equally striking is the fact that in spite of many reports in the Gospels of caustic criticism of Jesus, there is no instance recorded of women being hostile to him.

It seems that women joined the crowd who followed him without having been specially "called," and moved about the country with him even though his day-to-day life was hazardous and often deficient in the customary amenities. In light of the Palestinian custom of women being married near the age of puberty, and in view of the danger that parents would surely have seen in allowing single daughters to live with men, it may be assumed that all the women in Jesus' band had married. Some may have been widows, but some were probably wives of his male disciples. Luke reports that on one occasion Jesus sent out several dozen pairs of disciples into Palestine to proclaim the "kingdom of God,"[3] and there is no reason to think the mission may not have been at least partly composed of husband and wife teams. From information given by Paul and Luke it seems that travel by married couples was later a known pattern of mission activity among the apostles and other Christian teachers.[4] In addition to providing for the needs of their spouses, the women probably functioned as evangelistic copartners. Priscilla, for example, along with her husband instructed the well-educated Apollos so that he would know the Christian tradition more accurately.[5] And an early church father suggested that the apostles took wives along "that they might be their fellow-ministers in dealing with housewives. It was through them that the Lord's teaching penetrated also the women's quarters without any scandal being aroused."[6]

Women followed Jesus not only when his gospel drew popular acclaim. It is significant that when the cost of discipleship was high the women showed a faithfulness and courage the men lacked. If there is a "weaker sex," then the crucifixion scene suggests that the female followers who unflinchingly stood by do not belong to it. Luke indicates that a number of women were not afraid to identify with Jesus even after he had been condemned to be executed as a common criminal. "Great numbers of people followed, many women among them, who mourned and lamented over him. Jesus turned to them and said, 'Daughters of Jerusalem do not weep for me; no, weep for yourselves and for your children.' "[7] Transcending his own intense suffering, Jesus gave in these words an appropriate final comment on the sad plight of his society and of women in particular. Realizing that their lot would probably not improve in the future, he counseled them to prepare for the difficult days ahead. Peter Abelard, noting that women at that crucial time showed more fidelity than Peter, "the Prince of the Apostles," finds in their action an illustration of Paul's description of the height of devotion. Abelard appropriately applied the lyric words which begin: "Who shall separate us from the love of Christ? Shall tribulation or distress?"[8]

Is there any special or particular reason to account for the fact that many women were attracted to the person and the gospel of Jesus? Was it mainly because women tend to value peace and security highly, and appreciated a man who rejected the militant Zealots' advocacy of violent revolt against Rome? Was it partly because women like a man who is kind to children, and they were charmed by his way with youngsters? Or is there some other reason?

## THE STATUS OF HEBREW WOMEN

Jesus grew up in a culture whose estimate of women was lower than it had been in an earlier time. His Jewish contemporary Philo wrote, "Man is informed by reason; woman by sensuality."[9] In that same century Josephus claimed, "In every respect woman is inferior to man."[10] A rabbinic prayer of that era—similar to one still used in daily worship by Jewish orthodoxy—read: "Blessed be Thou for not having made me a gentile, a woman, or an ignoramus."[11] Another derogatory beatitude is recorded in the Talmud: "Blessed is he whose children are males, and woe to him whose children are females."[12] Because of judgments such as these, Albrecht Oepke rightly observes that by contrast with earlier Israelite attitudes the status of woman in the Judaism of Jesus' day "involves more reaction than progress."[13]

Scripture was interpreted so as to make women look worse than depicted in the creation stories. Jesus ben Sirach, for example, who lived two centuries before Jesus ben Joseph, regarded Adam's spouse as the root of all evil. In one of the earliest interpretations of the Garden of Eden story on record he charged: "Women is the origin of sin, and it is through her that we all die. Do not leave a leaky cistern to drip or allow a bad wife to say what she likes. If she does not accept your control, divorce her and send her away." That writer went on to claim: "Out of clothes comes the moth, and out of woman comes wickedness. A man's wickedness is better than a woman's goodness; it is woman who brings shame and disgrace."[14]

Jesus did not use Eve as the target of antifeminine criticism. He seems to have interpreted the Garden of Eden story in the way originally intended. The person who composed that story probably did not consider Eve more culpable than Adam. Both knew of the prohibited tree, but Adam put up less resistance to temptation than his mate. When offered the fruit he simply took it without qualm and swallowed it! Jesus endorsed the position of the originator of that profound story of Everyman and did not consider that male domination in history was intended by the Creator. According to Genesis 3 the rule of man over woman has come about as a result of human sin. However, in the ideal created order the wife does not have a servile status.

Translators of the Eden account have not made it clear that woman was not created to wait on man. In that story *azar* is unfortunately often rendered "helper." The English term is usually associated with a subservient position, but throughout Jewish Scriptures *azar* refers to either a superior or an equal—never to an inferior. According to the Genesis story woman was created from man's rib as an equal partner. A hymn of Charles Wesley captures well the status of woman suggested there.

> Not from his head was woman took,
> As made her husband to o'erlook;
> Not from his feet, as one designed
> The footstool of the stronger kind;
> But fashioned for himself, a bride,
> An equal, taken from his side.[15]

Males have commonly misinterpreted woman's creation from man's "rib" to mean that she is an insignificant side issue or an afterthought. But Robert Grimm, who rejects the bigotry that exalts superior Adam, has commented that "the woman is not his creation. While she was being fashioned out of him, he was sound asleep! She is his helper, certainly, but not primarily in order to serve him, or even to collaborate with him; her function is to enable him to achieve, with her, their true humanity."[16]

The Eden story was composed by someone who believed that woman's inferior role has come about through the disruption of God's purpose. It tacitly affirms monogamy as the divinely intended marital arrangement, in referring to the two becoming "one flesh." Polygamy, with its lowering of a wife's equal status, first appears with Lamech, a murderer more despicable than his ancestor Cain.

Jesus carried forward the concern for dignifying the role of woman articulated in the Genesis creation stories. He did more than any other biblical personality to put into practice the view that females and males are equal before God. How did he raise the status of women? His rejection of the double standard in sexual morality was one prominent way. A woman received harsher treatment for sexual infidelity than a man, even though the law of Moses prescribed that both participants in adultery should suffer the death penalty.[17] To frighten a confession from such a woman she was dressed in black and brought to the eastern Temple gate. The priest humiliated her by untying her hair and tearing her dress so that her bosom was publicly exposed.[18] Then he required her to drink a magic potion concocted by mixing holy water with dust from the sanctuary and with ink from the scroll on which the accusation against her was written. If guilty "her face turns yellow and her eyes bulge and her veins swell" and she has a miscarriage.[19] If she suffered no physical damage from that terrifying psychological ordeal, her innocence was presumed to have protected her.

By contrast to this "bitter water" test administered to half-naked women by pitiless priests, Jesus believed it was unjust to treat punitively only one party to a liaison. Thus when some men alleged that a couple had been detected in "the very act of adultery," he probably realized that the Pharisees were zealous to prosecute only one of the partners whose sin was witnessed. To these men Jesus said, "Let him who is without sin among you be the first to throw a stone at her."[20] He dealt sternly with the self-righteous male accusers and gently with the adulterous woman—although he did not condone her behavior.

Editorial prudery is probably the reason why that episode of Jesus with the wrathful men and the adulterous woman barely survived in early Christian authoritative writing. Critics agree that it is probably authentic but realize that in style and in content it does not belong in John 8, where it is usually found in translations. The story is omitted from some of the chief ancient manuscripts and is attached at various points in others. In style and content it best fits after Luke 21, where some ancient editors have placed it. Jesus' leniency toward that wayward woman appears to have been too iconoclastic for the postapostolic community. Church leaders who condemned sexual laxity found his teaching subversive. Textual critic C. K. Barrett suggests that the story had difficulty in achieving canonical status not because of doubtful authenticity but because it "seemed inconsistent with the strict disciplinary treatment of adultery then customary."[21]

Elsewhere in the Fourth Gospel is the account of another encounter with an adulteress. Jesus' conversation at Jacob's well illustrates his unconventional openness toward women who had engaged in illicit sexual relations. Jewish religious leaders would normally have considered the person found there drawing water unworthy of notice for three reasons: she was a woman, an adulteress, and a Samaritan. Jesus' associates were upset at his willingness to waste time discussing theology and morality with a woman, especially one they regarded as a half-breed heretic and a social outcast. Of this G. F. Moore says, "The surprise of the disciples of Jesus, as narrated in John 4:27, at finding their master talking with a woman was quite in accord with rabbinical ideas of propriety."[22]

Devout Jewish men felt that purity had been sullied if women of ill repute were treated with kindness. For example, Philo's judgment on prostitutes was harsher than the Mosaic law. He called them "a pest, a scourge, a plague to the public" and advised that they be stoned to death.[23] The admonition of Jesus ben Sirach was typical: "Do not go near a loose woman for fear of falling into her snares."[24] The concern expressed here is not for the restoration of a lewd person, but only for saving oneself by avoiding anyone thought to be unchaste.

Robert Leslie claims that the interpersonal relations depicted in the Jacob's well episode were profoundly therapeutic because Jesus accepted the woman of Samaria as a person while rejecting her self-destructive behavior. He comments on Jesus' response to the woman's defensiveness:

He refused to reject her as she rejected him; but he refused, also, to allow her to dictate the terms of their relationship. Refusing to move away from her and her predicament, he nevertheless took the topic of conversation offered to him, redirected it into an area of personal relevance for her, and related her need to a larger dimension that included God. . . . The only way to the kind of life that held real meaning for her ("living water") was to clear up the moral problem which made impossible a true relationship either with her fellow human beings or with God. . . . Her invitation to others to talk with Jesus is the best possible proof of the effectiveness of his ministry to her.[25]

Also Jesus rejected the divorce law of his culture, in part no doubt because men had flippantly exploited it and because it was exclusively a male perogative. Hillel, the celebrated Jewish scholar at the time of Jesus' birth, asserted that a husband had the right to divorce his wife "even if she spoiled a dish for him."[26] The Mishnah also states that a wife can be "put away with her consent or without it."[27] No hearing was required before a court of justice. The disgruntled husband had only to hand her a *get* paper and tell her to get out! Yet a wife could not divorce her husband even if he were cruel and lecherous.

It is clear that, by contrast, Jesus saw unfairness in a system of divorce as the right of only one sex. He acknowledged the Roman practice which permitted either spouse to initiate a divorce.[28] But he held that it was equally morally wrong for either party to exercise this legal right. Like Hosea, he maintained that partners should conduct themselves as the forgiving God of Israel acts toward his people. He does not break covenant when offended, so neither should a husband and wife who are joined by God reject one another on any ground whatever.[29]

A double standard of sexual morality was also expressed in the Jewish culture: polygyny was permitted but not polyandry. Although monogamy had been the usual marital pattern, polygyny was practiced by some Israelite patriarchs, kings, and commoners. In the period in which Jesus lived, for example, Herod the Great had many wives. Citing the creation account in which monogamy is assumed, Jesus showed that he did not sanction polygamy of any type. In response to a question about divorce Jesus answered, "Have you never read that the Creator made them from the beginning male and female? . . . For this reason a man shall leave his father and mother, and be made one with his wife; and the two shall become one flesh."[30]

There are several other subtle but telling ways in which Jesus subverted the antifeminism of his day. First, he avoided the chronic male proclivity toward stereotyping women. There is no instance of Jesus cautioning men about the wiles of women. Rather, he viewed all humans as individuals, without classifying behavior as masculine or feminine. Second, in his teaching Jesus had no reluctance to draw examples from situations involving either sex. Parables with a primary focus on women are those of the leaven, the ten maidens, the lost coin, and the unjust judge, which show that he empathized with various situations faced by women. Third, Jesus attempted to counteract economic discrimination against women. He was angered by those who pretend to be faithful Jews but "devour widows' houses."[31] And his concern for the plight of widows is reflected in one of his parables.

There was once a judge who cared nothing for God or man, and in the same town there was a widow who constantly came before him demanding justice against her opponent. For a long time he refused; but in the end he said to himself, "True, I care nothing for God or man; but this widow is so great a nuisance that I will see her righted before she wears me out with her persistence."[32]

Jeremias has provided some clarifying comments about this parable. "Since the widow brings her cause to a single judge, and not before a tribunal, it would appear to be a money-matter: a debt, a pledge, or a portion of an inheritance, is being withheld from her. She is too poor to bribe the judge . . . hence persistence is her only weapon."[33]

In a variety of ways Jesus showed that he was devoted to carrying out the full implications of the doctrine that all men and women are made in the image and likeness of God. Harry E. Fosdick aptly described Jesus' winsome outlook toward women in this way: "He treated women as he treated men—as persons sacred in their own right, as souls loved of God and full of undisclosed possibilities. He never condescended to women, but habitually showed them deference, and to the surprise of the attendant audience more than once came to their spirited defense."[34] Dorothy Sayers also has displayed keen insight on why women were especially drawn to Jesus:

They had never known a man like this Man . . . who took their questions and arguments seriously; who never mapped out their sphere for them, never urged them to be feminine or jeered at them for being female. . . . There is no act, no sermon, no parable in the whole Gospel that borrows its pungency from female perversity; nobody could possibly guess from the words and deeds of Jesus that there was anything "funny" about woman's nature.[35]

Thus it is apparent that one main reason why ordinary men and women found Jesus personally magnetic was because he respected them primarily as humans and only secondarily as male and female. He ranked persons by service but not by sex. He stated paradoxically that those who would be first must be last of all and servant of all. By that standard women have throughout history certainly qualified at least as well as men for preeminence in the earthly and heavenly Kingdom of God.

## WOMEN PROMINENT IN JESUS' LIFE

We have looked broadly at Jesus' relations with women generally—let us now study the particular women we know of his life. Due
to the impact of church tradition it is difficult to weigh the comparative significance of individual women. In Catholicism Mary of
Nazareth has been crowned "Queen of Heaven" and has partially
eclipsed the other merely mortal women of the Gospels. It is one of
the ironies of history that the woman whom Jesus in no way exalted
has been proclaimed "Coredemptress." Jesus' first recorded words
contain a mild rebuke to his mother. She had reproached her twelve-
year-old for staying behind in Jerusalem and spending his time with
scholars at the Temple. Jesus wondered at his parents for not understanding his religious interests or realizing how absorbed he was in
conversing with learned rabbis inaccessible to him in his home town.
It is apparent from Luke's account that he had already gone beyond
the intellectual and spiritual depth of his simple parents.[36]

Elsewhere in Luke's Gospel Jesus criticized a woman who praised
his mother. She had exclaimed, "Blessed is the womb that bore you
and the breasts that you sucked!" Jesus rejected her sentimentalism
by replying sharply, "Blessed rather are those who hear the word
of God and keep it!"[37] A similar response was given by Jesus when
his mother and brothers, who thought he was "beside himself,"
wanted to rescue him from mounting opposition in Galilee. He was
undaunted by the ruptured bond with his family and claimed that the
deepest relationships of life are not kinship ties. "My mother and
brothers are those who hear the word of God and act on it," he
asserted.[38]

The Fourth Gospel portrays some ambivalence in the relationship
of Jesus with his mother. At the beginning of his ministry, on turning
to him for help in a practical matter, she received a curt reply: "O
woman, what have you to do with me?" However, at the end of his
ministry Jesus was considerate enough of his mother to arrange for
her care after his death.[39]

According to Mark, the most memorable tribute that Jesus gave
any person was spoken of a woman. He said of one whom the Fourth
Gospel identifies as Mary of Bethany, "Whenever in all the world
the gospel is proclaimed, what she has done will be told as her

memorial."[40] But let us now look at the context of this commenda-
tion and of other eposides which display depth of sensitive feeling
between Jesus and Mary.

It was Mary's anointing that prompted the tribute just quoted.
Also evoked by the act was Jesus' remark, "She has done a beautiful
thing to me,"[41] in response to his disciples' criticism of her generous
gift. For she had poured upon him nard ointment from an alabaster
jar. This was an import from India valued at three hundred denarii
—a year's wages for a Palestinian laborer. The disciples were ostensi-
bly disgusted at her lavishing on Jesus a product which might have
been sold and the proceeds distributed to the poor. Doubtless they
assumed that Jesus shared their view, since he denounced luxurious
living and was concerned for the economically deprived. But he
probably perceived that they were not so much indignant over the
stewardship principle involved as ruffled by the fact that an immod-
est woman with loose hair should be received without reserve by
their leader. That there was depth of feeling between Jesus and Mary
is suggested by the degree to which he apparently felt at home in
Bethany, where Martha and Lazarus were also his friends. Judging
from the Gospel records, he rested there more often than in any
other place during his public ministry outside Galilee, staying with
them when he was in the vicinity of Jerusalem.[42]

What was the nature of the anointing custom in which Mary
engaged when Jesus ate dinner in Bethany? Anointing guests was a
common Jewish expression of hospitality. In the incident at the
house of Simon the Pharisee, Jesus responded to implied criticism
of himself by noting that his host had omitted that gracious act.[43]
Like the psalmist, he felt courtesy and comfort in the gesture: "Thou
preparest a table for me. . . . Thou anointest my head with oil.
. . ."[44] Ointments, usually of olive oil base, were poured or rubbed
on parts of the body to give ease. Palestine was often hot and dry;
an ointment soothed and protected the skin. Since soap was unknown in antiquity, it also to some extent served as an emollient. It
was often perfumed for additional pleasure, for men as well as
women.[45]

But it would have been out of character for Jesus to extol Mary's
action if it did no more than give him a delightful massage such as
the well-to-do could afford. Also customary at this period was the

preparation of ointments for funeral rites.[46] Unlike Jesus' unperceptive male disciples, Mary seems to have had some depth of awareness of the personal danger he was facing due to his having attempted to rid the temple of commercialization. The powerful priestly party would surely succeed in disposing of him. In view of this predicament Jesus explained: "You always have the poor with you, and whenever you will, you can do good to them; but you do not always have me. She has done what she could; she anointed my body beforehand for burying."[47]

What further is known of the woman who, according to Mark, Matthew, and John, anointed Jesus in Bethany, and who in the Fourth Gospel is identified as Mary the sister of Martha? Luke 7:- 36–50 and 10:38–42 contain two stories which may refer to her, although her identity in the first episode must be guessed. In this incident at the home of Simon the Pharisee, in some community not named, Luke describes how while Jesus ate dinner "a woman of the city who was a sinner" came in and poured out her love for him. Her unbound tresses displayed her flagrant disregard for the strictures of Jewish oral tradition.[48] She was probably a prostitute who felt guilty for having flaunted the moral code of her culture. Jesus was impressed by her profuse display of repentance and personal affection.

A number of ancient and contemporary scholars regard that Lukan episode as a variation of the Bethany anointing story.[49] In composing the narrative regarding the last days of Jesus' ministry, Luke probably omitted Mark's story of an anointing at a certain Simon's home in his borrowings from that Gospel because he thought it duplicated what he had inclined earlier.

Further on in Luke is another story involving women identified as Mary and Martha. The unnamed village which provides the setting may have been Bethany, and Martha, the officious hostess, may possibly have been the wife of Simon, the host at the dinner described earlier. She was intent upon fulfilling the traditional housekeeper role and thus much preoccupied with food preparation. Martha was disturbed that her sister longed for experiences beyond the domestic routine. Possibly she thought Mary was behaving in a presumptuous way. But Jesus encouraged Mary to reject the notion that "anatomy is destiny" and to realize that a woman could be something other than a homebody. He admired her eagerness for learning and, in effect, informed Martha that Mary should not be criticized for seeking to be liberated from the limitations of her culturally defined role. In that society a woman was admired principally for her abilities in food preparation and baby production. Jeremias, in his *Jerusalem in the Time of Jesus,* has this to say with respect to the place of the Jewish woman: "She is chiefly valued for her fecundity, kept as far as possible shut away from the outer world, submissive to the power of her father or husband."[50]

Mary was in violation of social mores when she "sat at the Lord's feet and listened to his teaching."[51] This was in fact a customary posture for a student; Luke later speaks of Paul being educated "at the feet of Gamaliel."[52] Mary rebelled against what is now described as "the feminine mystique"—the notion endemic to human culture that a woman's fulfillment is inseparable from her homemaking role.[53] She was a forerunner of Susan B. Anthony, who exclaimed, "What an absurd notion that women have no intellectual and moral faculties sufficient for anything but domestic concerns!"[54] Engaging in an interpersonal learning situation with a wonderful and intriguing rabbi took priority for Mary over hustling to serve him a fancy meal. The taboo normally surrounding any such discussion is seen in the disdainful comments of ancient rabbis, one of whom gravely warns: "The man who prolongs conversation with a woman does himself harm, and wastes the time he should be putting on the study of the Torah, and in the end will occupy a place in hell."[55] Another enjoins: "Let the words of the Torah burn up but let them not be transmitted to a woman."[56] Over against this prevailing attitude, Jesus said of one who aspired to something more challenging than the humdrum of preparing dinner and washing dishes: "The part that Mary has chosen is best, and it shall not be taken away from her."[57]

The best known of Jesus' female friends is Mary Magdalene. Since the name Mary was as common then as now, this woman is usually identified in the Gospels by the double name. To avoid confusion we will refer to her simply as Magdalene. That name was in token of her having come from Magdala, a fishing town along the Sea of Galilee. It was only a few miles from Capernaum, the town Jesus most often frequented during his Galilean ministry. It was possibly when he came to Magdala by boat that Magdalene became aware of him.[58] She was attracted to him by his reputation as a healer, for she had a severe psychic disorder. After Jesus exorcised the "seven demons" with which she was possessed,[59] she became his devoted follower. Mark informs his readers that Magdalene was among the women who waited on Jesus and took care of his needs when he was in Galilee, and accompanied him to Jerusalem.[60] She was among those brave and loyal women who remained with Jesus throughout the crucifixion. Whereas his obtuse and uncomprehending male disciples deserted him during that last day,[61] she was with him until the agony was over. She saw where his body was buried and returned to that place with ointments and spices after the sabbath was over.

Although Magdalene had a notable place among Jesus' female followers during his public ministry, she is most remembered for her Easter testimony. The distinguished New Testament authority C. H. Dodd expresses the view of many scholars and laymen when he refers to it as "the most humanly moving of all the stories of the risen Christ."[62]

What was the nature of that experience? Some have psychologized Magdalene's encounter with the resurrected Jesus as a hallucination triggered by grief. According to that view, the death of her lover on a hideous instrument of torture caused her to regress into the fantasy realm that was characteristic during her period of mental unbalance before meeting Jesus. In one of the earliest reflections of Jesus' resurrection, Celsus the Jew attempted to debunk the alleged occurrence by assuming that it happened to a woman in delirium. He claimed that many in such a state have had apparitions stimulated by wishful thinking.[63]

Ernest Renan, the famed French biblical critic of the last century, has eloquently presented the view that the so-called resurrection of Jesus was nothing more than the imagining of Magdalene's disordered mind. He portrays a woman frantic over the loss of the man she adored.

Mary alone loved enough to pass the bound of nature and revive the ghost of the perfect master. The glory of the resurrection belongs, then, to Mary Magdalene. After Jesus, it is Mary who has done the most in the founding of Christianity. The image created by her vivid susceptibility still hovers before the world. She, as chief and princess among visionaries, has better than any other made the vision of her impassioned soul a real thing to the world's conviction. That grand cry from her woman's heart, "He is risen!" has become the mainspring of faith to mankind. Hence, feeble reason, test not by cold analysis this masterpiece of ideality and love![64]

Romanticist Renan summarizes the Easter experience tersely: "It was love that raised Jesus again."[65]

Few Christians have found the hallucination theory of the resurrection adequate. Most find it overly reductionist to suppose that the Christian church was begun by a postmortem fiction manufactured by the emotional needs of one or more of Jesus' disciples. The traditional interpretation of Magdalene's experience is that her longing contributed nothing to Jesus' being raised from the dead. Numbed by grief, she came to his tomb intending to anoint with funeral perfumes the body of Jesus, which had been hastily buried without the customary treatment on the eve of the sabbath. While in that passive mental state she was unexpectedly greeted by Jesus, whom God had raised as a corporeal person. The traditionalist has held that the corpse of Jesus was reanimated by a miracle, in a somewhat transformed state, and that it was exclusively at the initiative of the risen Lord that Magdalene's fear and disbelief were changed into belief.

The naturalist interpretation—stressing the resurrection as a phenomenon wholly within the mind of Magdalene—and the supernaturalist interpretation—stressing the resurrection as a revived fleshly organism which anyone present could discern with his senses —both seem implausible to me. Neither position does full justice to the dominant note sounded by the New Testament witness to the resurrection. Magdalene's experience is probably best understood as a combination of internal and external factors.

The blend of objective revelation with subjective awareness can be seen by comparing Magdalene's resurrection experience with that of the apostle Paul. Her exclamation, "I have seen the Lord!" parallels Paul's query, "Have I not seen Jesus Christ our Lord?"[66] He was probably referring to what Luke describes as Paul's "vision" of a risen Lord on the road to Damascus.[67] The apostle testified to the Corinthians in the earliest record of the resurrection that Christ "appeared" *(hophthen)* to him. The verb he used to describe that firsthand experience is frequently used of theophanies in the Septuagint and elsewhere in the New Testament.[68] Job, for instance, confesses after encountering the Lord in the whirlwind, "Now I *see* thee."[69] Isaiah also says, "I *saw* the Lord sitting upon a throne."[70] That prophet used visual, auditory, and tactile metaphors to describe a supraempirical mystical experience.

On the assumption that God exists, disclosures of that Being are real occurrences. Seen in this light, Magdalene's Easter experience was not a self-induced hallucination. Although she did not dream up the presence of Jesus, neither was the event a "bolt out of the blue" for which there was no inward preparation. Perhaps close ties with Jesus over a period of years gave her a readiness to believe that the love she had known was not defeated. In the bewilderment that followed Jesus' death Magdalene was probably desperately attempting to reconcile his crucifixion with what he had taught her about his mission, human sin, and God's will. She may have been trying to puzzle through all of this as she went to visit Jesus' tomb. There she had a deeply moving experience which resulted from the divine initiative quickening her mind. After "seeing" Jesus and "hearing" him call her name she became convinced that he was not dead but altogether alive, although in a different mode.

The changed nature of the relationship is expressed in Jesus' words to Magdalene, "Do not continue to hug me" *(me mou haptou).*[71] The verb *haptou,* used only here in the Fourth Gospel, ranges in meaning in the New Testament from making contact with a garment to having intercourse with a partner.[72] The verbal tense here with the negative means to cease an action in which one has been engaged. This imperative graphically symbolizes the traumatic transformation to which Magdalene was adjusting as her tie with Jesus became exclusively intangible. No longer could she take hold of him physically, for he was no longer incarnate. John Marsh, in a recent commentary, has given this perceptive interpretation: "What Jesus is doing and saying to Mary can be summed up thus: She is to cease from holding him, because the new relationship between Lord and worshipper will not be one of physical contact, though it will be a real personal relationship."[73]

There are insights on the resurrection expressed elsewhere in the New Testament which reinforce this interpretation. Paul stated: "If we have known Christ according to the flesh yet now no longer we know him." Also he told the Corinthians that both transformation and continuity were involved in the resurrection of a person. "It is sown a physical body, it is raised a spiritual body."[74] Paul was faithful to Jesus' interpretation of life after death. In responding to a question on this subject Jesus asserted that the resurrected life is radically different from the conditions necessary for existence on earth.[75] No reanimation of the flesh is needed, for there is no biological functioning. Rather, those who are raised resemble angels, who were presumed to be immaterial.[76] Intercourse between loved ones in the resurrection is more intimate than is possible in our earthly association—"closer than hands or feet or the air we breath."

Magdalene was convinced that Jesus was alive and that her relationship with him was more personal and permanent than ever. She had come to believe that the triumphant Jesus was saying to his disciples, "I am with you always."[77] Moreover, she felt constrained to share rather than to hoard privately the disclosure that had converted her sorrow to gladness. Thus she related the revelation she had received to the other followers of Jesus, but evidently only some women accepted her story as true. Magdalene and the other women who had been with her at Jesus' tomb faced male prejudice when they testified of Jesus' living presence. The apostles dismissed their story as nonsense.[78] The response is understandable when we realize that a woman's witness was discounted as worthless in the ancient Palestinian culture. Josephus, for instance, says, "Let not the testimony of women be admitted."[79]

The embarrassment of men in later centuries over Magdalene's testimony is reflected in some translations of John 20:17. The common English translation, "Touch me not!" follows the Vulgate, *"Noli me tangere!"* These translations make it appear that Jesus issued a cold, forbidding command in response to Magdalene's spontaneous gestures of affection. Were these translations correct, it would seem that the composer of John 20 believed Jesus to have had a phobia against women feeling him while encouraging men to touch him. According to John 20:27 Jesus shows his hands and his side and invites Thomas to put his hand on those bodily parts.

It is unfortunate that Western readers of the resurrection accounts generally think that Jesus greeted Mary with an austere prohibition, for it is probably far removed from what the original Greek writer was attempting to convey. *Me mou haptou* signified that the physical relations that she had previously had with Jesus and which she desired to continue were no longer appropriate or possible in the resurrected life.

Looking back, what relationship does there seem to be between the women prominent in Jesus' life? The anointing-by-a-woman stories which are found in all the Gospels have been examined. It was argued that those stories probably refer to a single episode pertaining to a woman identified in the Fourth Gospel as Mary the sister of Martha. This would mean that Jesus and a repentant prostitute mutually loved one another and delighted to be in one another's company. The information about Magdalene was also analyzed. The only episode about that woman whom Jesus cured of a personality disorder occurs after Jesus' death.

Magdalene and the sister of Martha are probably not two different characters. Identification of the two is favored by some scholarly New Testament expositors.[80] Unless the stories associated with Jesus' friend named Mary are blended together, it is difficult to understand why the woman with whom Jesus was closest during his public ministry is not explicitly mentioned as being among the women present at the crucifixion or at the tomb on Easter morning. Likewise it is puzzling that Magdalene could be the most notable person at the crucifixion and at the resurrection of Jesus without there being some earlier episodes in which she was involved. Except for the conflicting towns of Magdala and Bethany with which the various stories are associated, there is considerable reason for coalescing them into an account referring to one person.

Form criticism has demonstrated that little historical importance can be given to the geographical setting of the vignettes recorded. The episodes of Jesus' life circulated orally for a generation after his death with little attention to locale. Those who wrote the Gospels strung together somewhat arbitrarily the stories about Jesus into a connected narrative. Although they attempted to organize the oral tradition on a broad geographical framework, they had few clues for locating accurately where various happenings took place or for establishing chronological sequence.

From at least as early as the second century there has been the common assumption that Magdalene was the penitent woman who wiped Jesus' feet with her hair.[81] In the art and literature of Western Catholicism this identification has persisted, and her acceptance by Jesus has been widely featured as the cardinal exhibit of his magnanimity.[82] Sensitive writers such as J. Middleton Murry, Sholem Asch, Dorothy Sayers, and Francois Mauriac find one composite figure in the accounts of women whom Jesus treated with special fondness.[83] Kahlil Gibran has offered a suggestive reconstruction of a reminiscence Magdalene might have had. Regarding Jesus she testified:

I gazed at him, and my soul quivered within me, for he was beautiful. . . . He said, "You have many lovers, and yet I alone love you. Other men love themselves in your nearness. I love you in yourself. Other men see a beauty in you that shall fade away sooner than their own years. But I see in you a beauty that shall not fade away, and in the autumn of your days that beauty shall not be afraid to gaze at itself in the mirror, and it shall not be offended. I, alone, love the unseen in you." On that day the sunset of his eyes slew the dragon in me, and I became a woman. . . .[84]

Those who reject the identification of Magdalene with the maudlin hussy sometimes do so on puritanical grounds. Embarrassed that the Gospels state that Magdalene, together with other women, followed Jesus about the country to see to his needs and hear his teaching, they are anxious to affirm that at least she was a virgin. They find it execrable to think of Jesus having companionship with and being massaged by an ex-prostitute. J. B. Mayor questions, "Would it not have been putting an additional stumbling-block in the way of the weak, if one of notorious character were known to be habitually in the company of the new prophet?"[85] Such revulsion to postulating that Jesus had close ties with a woman of bad reputation shows how scandalous Jesus' principle of accepting sexual offenders still is in our culture.

In Palestinian culture it was unheard of for an unattached woman to travel with a righteous man. Magdalene was probably not a camp follower, as she appears to be in *Jesus Christ Superstar*. In the recently discovered *Gospel of Philip*, which records a tradition at least as old as the second century, Magdalene is referred to as Jesus' spouse.[86] If that were the case it would explain why the earliest evangelists regard her as the most prominent woman beloved by him. In the Synoptic Gospels Magdalene is placed first in each listing of women, just as Peter heads the listings of the apostles.[87]

## CHRISTIANITY AND FEMINISM

For two millennia churchmen have studied the value commitments of the founder of Christianity. Yet there has been little widespread recognition and appreciation of his attitudes toward the feminine half of the human race. Sometimes those who are antagonistic toward Christianity have seen more clearly than those within the church that Jesus was woman's advocate. Emperor Julian, in an effort to restore Rome to paganism, lampooned Jesus for forgiving wayward women.[88] Friedrich Nietzsche, perhaps modern Christianity's most influential adversary, has acknowledged that in the basic sources of Christianity women and marriage are "treated with earnestness, with reverence, with love and confidence." Fascinated by what he considered to be the Oriental notion of treating women as confinable property, he was disgusted that a facet of the ethic of Jesus was to respect both sexes equally. Like Jesus, Nietzsche referred to the Garden of Eden story, but his "Antichrist" interpretation is altogether different:

God . . . wanders in a leisurely fashion round his garden; but he is bored. . . . What does he do? He invents man—man is entertaining. But behold, even man begins to be bored. . . . So forthwith he creates yet other animals —God's *first* mistake, for man did not think animals entertaining. . . . Consequently God created woman. And boredom did indeed cease from that moment—but many other things ceased as well! Woman was God's *second* mistake. Woman in her inmost nature is a serpent.[89]

Nietzsche's contention that Jesus advocated the preposterous notion of equality for women was followed by H. L. Mencken, who faulted the religion of Jesus because it "was highly favorable to women."[90] In the eyes of these male chauvinists Jesus would not have failed so miserably if he had despised women!

Scorn of women has been enough a part of church history so that Nietzsche and Mencken ought to have appreciated much of institutional Christianity even if they found Jesus disgusting. In his *History of Women*, John Langdon-Davies has judiciously contrasted Jesus' respect for women with the disrespect for women of some of the church fathers. "To read the early church fathers," he asserts, "is to feel sometimes that they had never heard of the Nazarene, except as a peg on which to hang their own tortured diabolism—as a blank scroll upon which to indite their furious misogyny."[91]

In both the Roman church and Protestantism women have been denigrated by church tradition and by the opinions of prominent leaders. Catholic Clara Henning, the only woman canon lawyer in the United States, has charged that "all our laws express a male culture, or rather, a subculture of celibate males who legislate on the basis of what they *imagine* women to be. Candidates for this celibate priesthood are taught that women are not only dumb but dirty: ritually impure, intellectually inferior, emotionally unstable, in perpetual subjection to men by divine ordinance."[92]

The extreme to which antifeminism has been expressed in Christendom is seen in the execution by churchmen of many women alleged to be witches. From the fourteenth to the eighteenth century throughout Europe there were a number of campaigns to ferret out and eliminate eccentric women. Also in New England theologian Increase Mather and his son were largely responsible for the witch-hunt craze at Salem.

Among the spokesmen for contemporary conservative Protestants there are also judgments very far from the attitude of Jesus. Otto Piper shares the stance of Karl Barth in alleging that the principle of male dominance is grounded in the highest authority. Confusing the position of the apostle Paul at his worst with biblical revelation at its best, Piper writes, "Why God assigned to the male sex the superior position is a moot question; . . . the wife who rebels against her husband's role as the responsible head must give account for her sin."[93] Anglican C. S. Lewis, one of the most widely read Christian writers of our century, claims that a married woman has an inferior sense of justice. It is therefore proper that the husband "has the last word in order to protect other people from intense family patriotism of the wife."[94] On the level of Protestant conservatism for the masses, Billy Graham expresses much the same position. He testifies that women are wonderful as long as they stay in their divinely ordained place beneath their husbands: "Wife, mother, homemaker —this is the appointed destiny of real womanhood."[95] Of course,

Jesus did not suggest that women should reject the homemaking role, but there is no evidence that he thought all fertile women should make childbearing the *sine qua non* of existence.

Churchmen who believe that Jesus sanctioned the subservient role of woman have been dominant in the Christian tradition. Thus it is understandable that Sheila Collins should make the damning appraisal that the church "has been the most culpable party in perpetuating what is at heart an unhuman, not to say ungodly, view of woman" as "frail and dependent and as somehow secondary to the male."[96] Not least in the ugly legacy has been the modern reference to menstruation as "the curse". Yet neither Jewish Scriptures nor Jesus refer to mankind's precipitous "fall" or to God's "curse" on woman.

Happily, a small resolute minority in the church have accepted the outlook of Jesus and have been pioneers in feminism during the past century. The first woman's liberation convention, held in 1848 at the Wesleyan Chapel, Seneca Falls, N.Y., was organized and attended by devout Christians. "All men and women are created equal," the key affirmation of a declaration written at the convention, is a paraphrase of Genesis 1:27. In the early days of the women's rights movement there were among the few masculine supporters such eminent clergymen as William Channing, Theodore Parker, and Thomas Higginson.[97] Susan B. Anthony, the most influential women's suffrage leader, cannot be understood apart from her Quaker conviction respecting "the Inner Light." Members of her denomination equate that Light with the vitalizing presence of the spirit of Jesus within, which all may possess regardless of sex. It is also noteworthy that one of the first groups to admit women into the professions were the Congregationalists. In 1853 Antoinette Brown became an ordained minister in that church. At the time of her death there were more than three thousand women clergy in the United States.[98]

In areas outside of Western civilization the ethic of Jesus is also contributing to the liberation of the oppressed feminine majority of the world's population. Christian missionaries in Africa and Asia have usually rejected the demeaning traditional role there assigned to women. They teach that a woman's lord and master should be God, not husband. While visiting tropical Africa some years ago I was appalled by the two-legged beast of burden frequently seen along the roads and in the fields: it was the human female—plowing gardens, harvesting crops, and carrying loads to market heavy enough to make a stevedore stagger. I recall one woman who was weighed down by an enormous banana stalk on her back and a plump baby at her breast. In rather typical fashion she was followed by her husband, carrying only a bottle of palm wine.

Many African missionaries have sought to promote sexual equality through encouraging parents to send both girls and boys to Christian schools. In some areas stout resistance has hampered this endeavor. Parents have found that marriages are not easily arranged for daughters unwilling to do most of the heavy agricultural work. Prospective husbands are wary of girls trained to behavior that deviates from the drudgery customarily expected of wives. The cultural effect of the missionaries' appeal to women is expressed by Elie Kedourie: "Christianity . . . worked a disruption of the traditional tribal hierarchy in a way in which its rival, Islam, so clearly a man's religion, did not."[99] When we realize the claim of the Koran that "Allah has made women subservient to men," and Mohammed's description of woman as "man's supreme calamity,"[100] it is understandable that his followers in Africa and Asia have had little compassion for the low position of women.

In India Christian missionaries effected decisive changes that raised the status of women. William Carey, the outstanding early Baptist missionary, detested the Hindu custom which obliged a widow to abandon herself to cremation on her husband's funeral pyre. Through his efforts and that of other Christians the burning of widows was prohibited by law and remarriage was sanctioned.[101] Kenneth Latourette summarizes the general influence of Christian missions on the status of women in India thus:

Persistent efforts to alter the lot of women were a striking feature of the Christian enterprise. Schools were provided for girls. Numbers of pioneers among Indian women in furthering education for their sex were Christian. In consequence, in the twentieth century the literacy rate among Christian women was more than ten times that among their non-Christian sisters. . . . Missionaries fought the early marriage and the prostitution which bore particularly hard on women. . . . They discouraged polygamy.[102]

In other mission areas there was a parallel attack on antifeminism. In China, where Buddhism and Confucianism have provided the dominant ethical codes, there was opposition to those who championed Jesus' attitude toward women. The traditional attitude of the Chinese is well articulated in teachings ascribed to Buddha and Confucius. When a monk asked Gautama for advice on the proper conduct toward the opposite sex, this exchange ensued:

"What should be our attitude toward women?"

"Avoid the sight of them."

"But if we should see them, Lord, what must we do?"

"Do not speak to them."[103]

Confucius shared Buddha's depreciatory attitude toward women. "Women and underlings are most difficult to deal with," the sage testified. "If we are friendly with them they lose their deference."[104] Confucius regarded women as little more than breeding organisms and servants.

Madame Chiang Kai-Shek witnesses in her person and her writings to the transformation of values that has resulted from the Christian missionary effort. That daughter of a strong Christian mother has pointed out that missionaries stressed schooling for girls in a fashion unknown in traditional China. Several decades ago she wrote, "It is to the lasting credit of the missionaries that they used every means to get girls to study. Now these trained women are at the heart of many of the movements working to improve the living condition and the status of their sisters throughout the provinces."[105] Christians in China led the crusade for emancipating girls from the crippling practice of foot-binding. As regards this Tseng Pao-Swen has asserted: "Christianity does not envisage the woman as a mere toy for the man and is not afraid to tackle the problem of the bound feet. Christian girls were the first to be proud of natural feet instead of ashamed of them, and Christian boys were the first to marry them."[106] This statement by Miss Tseng, who headed a Chinese girl's school, is taken from her contribution to a symposium on "Christ and the World's Womanhood." In that symposium women leaders from Africa, China, Korea, Japan, India, South America, and the Philippines, as well as from Western countries testified as to ways in which the ethic of Jesus has dignified and elevated the status of women.

An examination of the life of Jesus has shown that, with regard to women, he made *de facto* their *de jure* status according to the creation doctrine of his culture. Wherever his spirit has deeply permeated our globe the true place of woman as man's equal has been acknowledged. Sociologist David Mace has rightly claimed: "Of all the world's great religious teachers, Jesus is unique in the respect he assigned to women as persons and in the extent to which he sought and enjoyed their companionship."[107] Unlike Confucius, Gautama, Hillel, Mohammed, and Aquinas—to single out only a few top-ranking religious geniuses of world culture—Jesus attempted to break the domestic-drudge mold in which woman has commonly been cast. Protestant theologian Harold Phillips' judgment is not an exaggeration:

In the liberation of womanhood, political, economic, social, is there any single factor that has had as much influence as the gospel of Jesus? He who immortalized the widow's mite, the woman with the box of ointment, the cottage of Bethany with its two sisters, Mary and Martha, he who spoke some of his noblest and profoundest words to an outcast woman at a well in Samaria has done more to liberate and redeem womanhood from servility, inferiority, and injustice than any other in history.[108]

Catholic theologian Leonard Swidler refers to Jesus as a revolutionary feminist and comments satirically, "It is an overwhelming tribute to man's intellectual myopia not to have discerned it effectively in two thousand years."[109] More positively Kenneth Woodward, in his article "From Adam's Rib to Women's Lib," concludes: "The Women's Liberation movement offers organized religion a unique opportunity to recover the authentic Biblical doctrine of the radical equality of men and women. It also provides the impetus for discovering Jesus' message of freedom from bondage—including sexual bondage."[110]

# 4

# *Ascetic Philosophers on Sexuality*

MUCH of the sexual outlook in Western civilization has been filtered through intellectuals who have championed moral dualism and its concomitant asceticism. That theory and associated practice is a legacy received mainly from the ancient Greek culture. Until this historical causation is recognized and its pervasive effects realized, it will be difficult if not impossible to see clearly the prevailing sexual viewpoint of participants in the biblical milieu.

The church was nurtured under the wing of the ancient Jewish culture, but before the young community had come of age the destruction of the Jewish state shifted its center of influence away from Jerusalem. As it moved westward and became predominantly Gentile, it attempted to assimilate radically different Hellenistic ideas about the body and the nature of ideal manhood. Although church leaders denounced those who believed that a perfect Jesus could not have been subject to the inevitable contamination that comes from being in the flesh, they tended to endorse as moral standards for Christians much of the widespread pagan asceticism. By the time the church was several centuries old it was permanently scarred by the stance of Mediterranean cults and philosophies that found no sanctity and much mischief in the physical.

The assumption that sexual abstinence is prerequisite to sublime purity was a pagan outlook shared by many common men and intellectuals of the Greco-Roman world and that viewpoint was projected onto earliest Christianity. From the third century onward it was believed that Jesus and his apostles were celibates, even though there is no reference to a celibate Jesus in the historical sources of Christianity and in spite of the fact that the New Testament states that wives traveled with the apostles, including the one who was the "rock" on whom the church was built.[1] Lifelong virginity was a plight to be lamented, not a condition giving distinction in holiness in the culture to which Jesus and his apostles belonged. Yet throughout most of the church's history, the pagan rather than the Jewish outlook on sexuality has been used to interpret the New Testament. Cardinal James Gibbons, for example, asserted that Jesus chose his mother and his apostles on the basis of their virginity. Moreover, after ascending on high, he selected a large band of virgin angels to surround his throne. That distinguished American Catholic concluded his amazing distortion thus: "Not only did our Lord thus manifest while on earth a marked predilection for virgins, but he exhibits the same preference for them in heaven."[2] Few would be surprised if a contemporary prelate living a century after Gibbons were to project a similar obsession with virgins onto the character of Jesus. Even though one New Testament letter writer makes marriage a requirement for church office, Catholic theologian J. W. Rehage compounds the error by stating that "many of the early clergy practiced celibacy by choice, after the example of Christ and most of the apostles."[3]

Church leaders have been heavily, if not consciously, influenced by pagan sexual asceticism, so it is germane to our study to examine a common perspective which many intellectual leaders of ancient Western culture had toward the body. The word *asceticism* comes from *askesis,* which first meant the training an athlete receives. The term has had a broad latitude of metaphorical meaning in philosophical literature. Some use the term as Socrates did—to designate the self-discipline needed for anyone desiring to become educated.[4] William James had reference to such moderate moral gymnastics when he referred approvingly to William Channing as an ascetic. That Unitarian minister rejected a life of ease and self-indulgence, but did not regard the sensuous life as defiling.[5] Since self-discipline is intrinsic to nearly all ethical philosophies, asceticism has usually been reserved to denote a more rigorous life-style. In the discussion that follows it will be used to refer to philosophies which maintain that the good life is achieved through renouncing all sensuous desires whose satisfaction is not essential for individual survival. The ascetic tends to believe that pleasures—especially those associated with sexuality—are detrimental to moral excellence.

Sexual asceticism was found in early Greek philosophy and it

became increasingly more prominent in the Greco-Roman civilization. As this side of classical culture is little admired in modern times,
little attention has been given to its impact. From the Renaissance
to the present day the Greeks have characteristically been associated
with an ethic of moderation. The judgments of two classical scholars
will be cited as evidence of this stereotype. In *The Greeks,* H. D. F.
Kitto has written: "Their standard, in all their activities, was a sane
balance. It is difficult to think of a Greek who can be called a
fanatic."[6] Edith Hamilton has also claimed: "Elsewhere, when the
desire to find liberation has arisen, it has very often led men to
asceticism and its excesses, to exaggerated cults bent on punishing
the body for corrupting the soul. This did not happen in Greece."[7]

Of course, from Homer onward the Apollonian slogan "Nothing
in excess" has been a major motif in the Greek culture. But studies
by Friedrich Nietzsche, Eric R. Dodds, and others have shown
movements to irrational extremes in some areas, including the area
of sexuality.[8] The sexual asceticism of Greek philosophy will now be
explored in a historical manner in order to detect its influence on
subsequent Western culture.

## GREEK PHILOSOPHY

Sexual asceticism was based on a moral dualism that can be traced
to the Orphic cult at the dawn of Western philosophy. A pun was
used in describing it: "The body *(soma)* is the tomb *(sema)* of the
soul." The followers of the legendary Orpheus also utilized a prison
metaphor: "The soul is undergoing punishment for sin and the body
is an enclosure or prison in which the soul is incarcerated."[9]

Pythagoras, the first Greek to call himself a philosopher, adopted
Orphic dualism in the sixth century B.C., and the fraternity he
founded extrapolated from it a metaphysical dualism. Females were
associated with qualities such as dark, evil, odd, and crooked.[10]
Although married, Pythagoras was reported to have said: "Keep to
the winter for sexual pleasures, in summer abstain; they are less
harmful in autumn and spring, but they are always harmful and not
conducive to health." Asked once when a man should consort with
a woman, he replied, "When you want to lose what strength you
have."[11]

Empedocles, a pupil of Pythagoras, denounced all forms of sexual relations.[12] Dodds, in discussing Empedocles, observes that sexual asceticism not only originated in Greece but "was carried by a Greek mind to its extreme theoretical limit."[13]

Democritus, an admirer of Pythagoras, did not approve of sexual activity.[14] In turn, his most famous disciple, Epicurus, maintained that "the pleasant life is not the product of . . . sexual intercourse with women."[15] Although he was maligned by rival schools as being a notorious lecher, he did not advocate unrestrained hedonism.[16] Rather he affirmed: "The wise man will not fall in love. . . . Sexual indulgence has never improved anyone. . . . The wise man will not marry and rear a family. . . . Occasionally, he may marry owing to special circumstances in his life."[17]

Lucretius, who popularized Epicurus' philosophy in the Latin culture, asserted that sexual desire was a sickness that could not be cured by coitus. A wise man should avoid it altogether, for it does not contribute to the ideal unruffled life. Instead of giving long-range serenity, it affords only a worthless brief respite. Lucretius described the problem in this way: "At length when the pent-up desire has gone forth, there ensues a short pause in the burning passion; and then returns the same frenzy, then comes back the old madness."[18]

Plato was indebted to the Orphic-Pythagorean cult for a number of his doctrines, not the least being that the body is a tomb from which one is emancipated by death. He believed that a human is an immaterial soul of psyche which can be temporarily trapped in an animal organism. Ontologically a man essentially *is* an eternal soul who incidentally *has* a temporal body.

The ideal man is pictured in the *Phaedrus* as one who has by self-mastery cured the disease of physical craving.[19] Although Plato was referring in that dialogue to abstinence from homosexual activity, "there is little in his writings to suggest that his revulsion from heterosexual intercourse was not equally strong."[20] Coitus had no humanizing aspects for Plato, so one who finds it pleasurable is compared to a "brutish beast."[21] In the *Phaedo* Plato's mouthpiece argues that a true philosopher does not concern himself with sexual pleasure.[22]

Plato writes in his last work, "Abstain from every female field in which you would not desire the seed to spring up."[23] B. A. G. Fuller interprets the meaning here to be: "All intercourse, even within the marriage bond, should be frowned upon unless it were for the express purpose of procreation." Fuller holds that for Plato "sex is inherently evil, its satisfaction on the physical plane is wantonness pure and simple, and is . . . the arch-enemy of the life of the spirit."[24]

Plato admitted that a woman may occasionally be suited for a role other than rearing children. Just as a bitch may serve as a fleet hunting dog, so a talented woman may be well suited for a responsibility outside the home. But he believed that women were generally inferior in spite of the fact that some individual women equaled or exceeded the competences of particular men.[25] Plato's low estimation of women is exposed in this reincarnation scale: "Of the men who came into the world, those who were cowards or led unrighteous lives may be with reason be supposed to have changed into the nature of women in the second generation."[26]

How can Plato, the acclaimed apostle of the harmonious life, be so severe toward the opposite sex and sexual passion? In the *Republic,* where he best expresses that moral philosophy, sexual desire is referred to as a diseased part of the personality.[27] In contrast to the appetite for food, which cannot be completely diverted or suppressed, Plato held that nature does not compel man to satisfy his sexual appetite and hence genital gratification is expendable.[28] He pictured the well-balanced person as one who sublimates all his amorous energies in intellectual pursuits.[29]

According to historian Crane Brinton, the intellectual in classical Greece tended to think of sex as "a nuisance, or at best an appetite likely to interfere with the conduct of life according to the Golden Mean."[30] In support of this statement he cites a comment of Sophocles which Plato recorded. When that playwright was asked if he still engaged in sexual intercourse, he responded: "It gives me great joy to have escaped the clutches of that savage and raging tyrant."[31] In that same passage sexual passion is referred to as *mania.*

Aristotle, the celebrated defender of the rational moral mean, rejected the position of those who expressed disdain for hedonism by pursuing a life devoid of pleasure.[32] However, he unwittingly aided the cause of future sexual asceticism by claiming that "a woman is a mutilated male."[33] Aristotle stated: "The male is by nature superior, and the female inferior; and the one rules, and the other is ruled. . . . The courage of a man is shown in commanding, of a woman in obeying. . . . The poet says, 'Silence is a woman's glory.' "[34] According to Aristotle, married couples may share the highest type of friendship *(philia).*[35] But Irving Singer comments on this relationship: "Friendship may exist between man and wife; but . . . it seems to be wholly independent of the emotional, sexual love for which Aristotle reserves the term *eros.*"[36]

Diogenes of Sinope, a contemporary of Aristotle, "praised those who were about to marry and refrained."[37] When that most picturesque representative of the Cynic school was asked about the proper time to marry, he quipped: "For young men, not yet; for old men, never."[38] Possibly he had learned from his hero Socrates that marriage could be an obstacle to the life-style of a philosopher. Xantippe, Socrates' wife, was a shrew who incessantly scolded her husband.[39] Diogenes was not against sexual expression but against the matrimonial institution that curbed living according to nature. Hence one of his mistresses was reputed to have been Laïs of Corinth, a famous prostitute of antiquity.[40] Augustine comments that Diogenes the Canine (or Cynic) philosopher copulated like a dog.[41]

Epictetus, one of the outstanding Stoics, sympathized with the Cynics who viewed marriage as a distraction from the ideal life, but he thought that sexual activity should also be renounced. His advice, "Endure and abstain," has been called "the keynote of later Stoicism."[42] In a chapter entitled "Concerning *askesis,*" Epictetus teaches that the impulse to indulge in drinking, eating, and sensual love should be counteracted by an opposing discipline of abstinence. The philosophic life and the ascetic life were almost synonymous for him. For that Stoic there are practical as well as theoretical reasons for the celibate life style. A husband has "to heat water for bathing the baby," he points out, "and when his wife has a child, provide wool, oil, a bed, and a cup—the vessels mount up at once—not to mention other business and distraction."[43]

The austere Stoic attitude toward women was articulated well by Epictetus. He wanted his disciples to beware of girls who have passed beyond the age of puberty, for their aim is nothing other than decorating themselves so as to seduce the opposite sex.[44] Enjoying the appearance of women was not advised for either the unmarried or the married. To the latter he whimsically admonished: "Do not admire your wife's beauty and you will not be angry when she commits adultery."[45] The Stoics held that "the passion of love is a craving from which good men are free; for it is an effort to win affection due to the visible presence of beauty." They continually preached that "the wise man is passionless *(apatheia)*" and classified love along with hatred and resentment as irrational conditions to shun.[46]

In the first century B.C. there was at Alexandria a revival of Greek philosophy. It was eclectic, the principal ingredients being Pythagoreanism, Platonism, and Stoicism. Knowledge of this eclecticism comes mainly from Philo, inasmuch as most of his writings have survived. Although a Jew, he was more influenced by Hellenistic culture than by rabbinic Judaism.[47] Regarding Philo an ancient historian has said, "It is on record that in his enthusiasm for the systems of Plato and Pythagoras he surpassed all his contemporaries."[48] That Philo shared the moral dualism of those Greeks can be seen in this exhortation: "Depart out of the earthly matter that encompasses you: escape, man, from the foul prison-house, your body, with all your might and main, and from the pleasures and lusts that act as its jailers."[49] Philo believed that mortification of the flesh was especially incumbent upon the lover of wisdom. He wrote:

The philosopher being a lover of what is virtuous cares for that which is alive within him, namely his soul, and disregards his body which is dead, having no other object but to prevent the most excellent portion of him, namely his soul, from being injured by the evil and death which is connected with it.[50]

Greek philosophers coming after Plato also contributed to Philo's sexual asceticism. He was indebted to Aristotle for the judgment that "the female is nothing else than an imperfect male."[51] The Stoics probably influenced Philo's belief that woman and man represent sensuality and intelligence respectively.[52] They also doubtless contributed to his doctrine that pleasure is the source of all evil.[53] Philo declared that salvation is achieved "not by moderation, but by the complete absence of passion *(apatheia)*."[54] During the first two centuries of the Christian era there flourished among the pagans a syncretism which is sometimes labeled Neo-Pythagoreanism. Wilhelm Windelband rightly calls it "a brand of eclectic religious Platonism."[55] Apollonius of Tyana, Numenius of Apamea, and Sextus were philosophers of that school. The celebrated Apollonius abstained from meat, wine, and women.[56] Numenius claimed that Pythagoras soundly believed that the physical stuff from which the world is created is evil and opposed to God. For Numenius individual salvation consisted in abandoning sexual activity so as to liberate the soul from passion.[57] Plutarch, writing about the same time as Numenius, mentioned certain philosophers who abstained from wine and women in order "to honor God by their continence."[58] He may have been referring to Neo-Pythagoreanism, for he was especially influenced by that School.[59] Sextus recommended castration as a protection against fornication. One of his maxims states: "You may see men cutting off and casting away parts of their body in order that the rest may be strong; how much better to do this for the sake of chastity."[60]

The era of ancient pagan philosophy came to an end around A.D. 300. C. H. Moore has shown that during its last several centuries "asceticism was the normal regimen for the philosopher of nearly every sect."[61] The Neoplatonists of the third century were only slightly less severe in scorning the passions than the Neo-Pythagoreans had been. Plotinus endorsed Plato's two forms of love, maintaining that one form pertained to "beauty itself" whereas the other form "seeks its consummation in some vile act."[62] This leading Neoplatonist held that the pure form of love "was not born of a mother and has no part in marriages."[63] Porphyry began his biography as follows: "Plotinus, the philosopher our contemporary, seemed ashamed of being in the body." Because of this embarrassment he rejected birthday celebrations.[64] A. H. Armstrong, an authority on Neoplatonism, describes Plotinus thus:

He seems to regard embodiment as a natural but regrettable necessity, rather as the Victorians regarded a visit to the W. C. His whole moral teaching is directed to so purify the soul that, though it must abide in body as long as its appointed term of embodiment lasts, yet it will live as though it were out of the body, utterly detached from material and earthly things.[65]

Porphyry was a faithful disciple of Plotinus, for he believed that coitus was defiling and that virginity was the *sine qua non* of purity.[66] Accordingly he praised some pagan Egyptian priests thus:

Chastity and purifications were common to all the priests. When . . . the time arrived in which they were to perform something pertaining to the sacred rites of religion, they spent some days in preparatory ceremonies . . . and during this time they abstained . . . above all, from a venereal connection with women.[67]

## MEDIEVAL PHILOSOPHERS

Gregory of Nyssa, an influential fourth-century Greek Christian, was a Neoplatonist.[68] He appropriated Plato's charioteer myth for describing the soul's descent and ascent.[69] It is soiled by sexual desire when it falls into the material realm, so the first stage in a return to perfection is achieved by a renunciation of marriage.[70] Bishop Gregory offered this advice: "A safe protective wall is the complete estrangement from everything involving passion."[71]

Augustine of Hippo, a younger Latin contemporary of Gregory, also had pagan asceticism woven into the fabric of his thought. He quoted with endorsement this sentiment of Cicero:

Should one seek the pleasures of the body, which, as Plato said truly and earnestly, are the enticements and baits of evil? What injury to health, what deformity of character and body, what wretched loss, what dishonor is not evoked and elicited by pleasure? Where its action is the most intense, it is the most inimical to philosophy. . . . What fine mind would not prefer that nature had given us no pleasures at all?[72]

To Augustine those questions of Cicero were especially poignant, for in his youth he habitually experienced with women what he called "the greatest of all bodily pleasures."[73]

Of all philosophies, Augustine was most fascinated with Neoplatonism. He internalized much of that outlook and consequently played a prominent role in moving Christianity toward what Nietzsche contemptuously called "Platonism for the people."[74]

As a result, in part, of studying Manicheanism and Greco-Roman philosophies during his formative years, Augustine came to assume that guilt feelings were normative even in marital expressions of sex. The common inclination to cover one's genitals in public and to prefer privacy and darkness for engaging in marital relations is offered as evidence that the sexual impulse is a sin and a shame.[75] Augustine was embarrassed to realize that the only external part of man's body that conscious will cannot regulate is the penis. He observed that it "sometimes refuses to act when the mind wills, while often it acts against its will."[76] He thus considered it quite proper to call the sexual organs indecent and dishonorable.[77] He admonished: "Detest these members as adultery is detested."[78] Augustine was among the first to relate sexual desires closely to original sin.[79] According to his theory of the seminal transmission of original sin, "everyone who is born of sexual intercourse is in fact sinful flesh."[80]

Augustine speculated on the way in which man's reason would have controlled his libido in the uncorrupted Eden. Stoic *apatheia* is predominant in his description of the copulation process:

Without the seductive stimulus of passion, with calmness of the mind and with no corrupting of the integrity of the body, the husband would lie upon the bosom of his wife. . . . No wild heat of passion would arouse those parts of the body. . . . The semen could have been introduced into the womb of the wife with the integrity of the female genital organ being preserved, just as now, with that same integrity being safe, the menstrual flow of blood can be emitted from the womb of a virgin. . . . Thus not the eager desire of lust, but the normal exercise of the will should join the male and female for breeding and conception.[81]

The ideal of passionless activity was an unrealized potentiality for Adam and Eve, but it has not been even a possibility for their descendants who are all genetically infected by the first parents' fall.

According to Augustine the closest approximation to passionlessness in worldly society is consecrated virginity. Consequently he advocated celibacy for all, cheerfully accepting the prospect that human history would quickly be ended if everyone took his advice.[82] Adolf Harnack has observed that "his *Confessions* are pervaded by the thought that he alone can enjoy peace with God who renounces all sexual intercourse."[83] Augustine claimed that the chosen people in ancient Judaism had no delight in sexual congress and "used marriage only for the sake of offspring." If they had lived after the advent of Jesus "they would have immediately made themselves eunuchs for the kingdom of heaven's sake."[84]

John Scotus Erigena was a ninth-century carrier of the Neoplatonic tradition. He translated Gregory of Nyssa's *Creation of Man* and was captivated by that work. Gregory, in turn, had been influenced by the androgynes myth of Plato's *Symposium,* according to which primal man was originally bisexual, and the male-female severance came as a result of punishment for sin.[85] Gregory transposed that story into the context of the Hebrew creation myths. The first human creation was in God's image and was therefore an immaterial ideal person. Potentiality for the inferior function of coitus came at a second stage of creation.[86] Gregory referred to sexual desire as a vice resulting from our corrupted nature.[87] Erigena likewise believed that the perfect image of God was in the mind of God as an idea without sexual differentiation.[88] It was because of sin that the original human was divided into the sexes.[89] He assumed that the male and the female are the embodiments of the intellectual and the sensual respectively.[90]

Thomas Aquinas' sexual attitudes show the direct and indirect impact of Greek philosophy. The celibate life is to be preferred because it is "unseared by the heat of sexual desire which is experienced in achieving the greatest bodily pleasure which is that of conjugal intercourse."[91] Anyone desiring to develop his rationality was advised by Aquinas to exclude coital distractions. He quoted with approval a confession of Augustine: "I feel that nothing so casts down the manly mind from its heights as the fondling of women and those bodily contacts which belong to the married state."[92]

The Angelic Doctor believed that strong sexual desire was evil even within the bonds of matrimony. Aquinas endorsed, as Jerome had earlier, this saying of Neopythagorean Sextus: "He who loves his own wife ardently is an adulterer."[93] Those who were married were informed by Aquinas that procreation could be accomplished without sin only if the participants functioned like ideal philosophers, under complete rational control. He admitted that heterosexual generation was intended by the creator, for he would certainly have given Adam a male associate if he had had pleasant companionship in mind. Aquinas, following Augustine, said of Eve, "She was not fitted to help man except in generation, because another man would have proved a more effective help in anything else."[94]

Aquinas followed Aristotle in believing that nature always wishes to produce a male, so a woman is a man gone wrong—a deformity that may have been caused by a moist south wind![95] Also he endorsed Aristotle's theory of reproduction in claiming that woman provides the passive matter whereas man supplies the active intelligible form.[96] The female role is compared to an inferior workman who prepares the material for the more skilled artist to shape.[97]

### MODERN PHILOSOPHERS

Immanuel Kant, Arthur Schopenhauer, and Søren Kierkegaard have been the only prominent philosophers since the Middle Ages to espouse sexual asceticism. It is unfortunate that none of them had a Catholic background, for they would probably have found the monastic community more satisfying than the lonely lives they led as bachelors.

Sexual desire was for Kant inextricably associated with shameful behavior, and this is the reason, he claims, why "all strict moralists, and those who had pretensions to be regarded as saints, sought to suppress and extirpate it." Kant believed that sexual desire "is a principle of the degradation of human nature, in that it gives rise to the preference of one sex to the other, and to the dishonoring of that sex through the satisfaction of desire."[98] He stigmatized connubial relations as mere animal copulation in his definition of marriage: "The union of two persons of different sex for life-long reciprocal possession of their sexual faculties."[99] Moreover, anyone who indulges in autostimulation of his genitals "degrades himself below the level of animals."[100]

Schopenhauer, a younger German contemporary of Kant, clarified his outlook in this way: "By the term asceticism . . . I mean in its narrower sense this intentional breaking of the will by the refusal of what is agreeable and the selection of what is disagreeable."[101] He prescribed the way that this ethic can best be accomplished: "Voluntary and complete chastity is the first step in asceticism."[102] He called the Augustinian doctrine of the transmission of evil by the procreative act a "great truth,"[103] and consequently admired those who had renounced the sexual life. "The inmost kernel of Christianity" is celibacy, according to Schopenhauer, because it curtails "the will to live" which is the central reality and the basic evil of the world.[104] He admired Jesus in that he is the "personification of the denial of the will to live."[105] He regarded the

Cynics and Jesus as forerunners of the "sublime institution" of monasticism and believed that the faithful monk's denial of the will to live superbly exemplified the only way to be saved.[106] Schopenhauer accepted the Stoic ideal of complete elimination of desire, but he did not share the Stoic optimism that man's reason could achieve this end.[107]

Like Augustine, Schopenhauer had difficulty bringing his sexual activity into line with the strenuous self-discipline dictated by his reason. Judging from the affairs he had with women (from whom he contracted syphilis), he found them physically irresistible.[108] But in his "Essay on Women" he expresses a fantastic psychological revulsion toward them. "The second sex is inferior in every respect to the first" is his theme in that famous literary monument of misogyny.

Kierkegaard referred to his older contemporary Schopenhauer as "a most significant author," but criticized him for advocating an asceticism that was not extremely demanding.[109] Both philosophers accepted the Augustinian doctrine of original sin and thought that the only way to halt its spread was by refusing to propagate.[110] Kierkegaard countered the criticism that the human race would perish if his viewpoint were generally accepted by saying, as earlier Augustine had, that such a loss would be no great misfortune.[111] The Danish philosopher thought of the libido as Pandora's box, filled with the basic ills of human existence, and he spent his life trying to keep the lid from popping open.

Kierkegaard's sexual revulsion resulted from some unusual experiences in early life as well as from ascetic strands in the tradition of Western philosophy. As a boy he discovered that he had been conceived illicitly while his father was married to someone other than his mother.[112] Also, as a youth, his dread of sex was increased by going to a brothel when intoxicated and fornicating.[113] P. P. Rohde sums up Kierkegaard's guilt-ridden attitude: "*The* sin par excellence is sexuality because the link with nature is here strongest."[114]

Identifying Christianity with struggle against natural urges, Kierkegaard saw no virtue in marriage.[115] The Christian, he believed, should always oppose the world, but "with marriage the Christian immediately has a different relation to the world than that of being a stranger and outcast, or salt, or being sacrificed, or putting a stop to things."[116] Convinced that God had called him to a life of celibacy, he suppressed his strong desire for marriage.[117] Thus he broke with his fiancée Regina precisely because his body cried out for sexual completion. He fancied that his renunciation of his sweetheart was parallel to Abraham's sacrifice of Isaac.[118] In both cases the universal moral imperative to provide offspring for forthcoming generations was suspended due to messages received by divine revelation.[119] But Kierkegaard also gave this rationale in support of opting for the single status: "God desires only one thing from us men—to be loved. But to love God a man must give up all egoism, and first and foremost the potentiated egoism of the propagation of the species, the giving of life. . . . So God wishes to have celibacy because he wishes to be loved.[120]

The Jewish philosopher Martin Buber has trenchantly argued that Kierkegaard's sexual asceticism, which is based on his proposition that "to love God is to hate what is human," is a desecration of the biblical ethic. He has commented:

Exclusive love to God ("with *all* your heart") is, *because he is God,* inclusive love, ready to accept and include all love. . . . "In order to come to love," says Kierkegaard about his renunciation of Regina Olsen, "I had to remove the object." That is sublimely to misunderstand God. Creation is not a hurdle on the road to God, it is the road itself. We are created along with one another and directed to a life with one another. . . . A God in whom only the parallel lines of single approaches intersect is more akin to the "God of the philosophers" than to the "God of Abraham and Isaac and Jacob." God wants us to come to him by means of the Reginas he has created and not by renunciation of them.[121]

Kierkegaard's last writings contain a shrill denunciation of marriage. Whereas in earlier works he thought of his single status as an exception to the universal duty of marriage, he came to view celibacy as the standard for the godly life, with marriage permitted for those who are incapable of continence.[122] He approved of Luther's rejection of a marital distinction between clergy and laity, but he applied the doctrine of the priesthood of all believers in this incredible manner: "It is not that the priest should be unmarried, but that the Christian should be unmarried."[123] He appealed to the alleged celibacy of Jesus as his ultimate support: "Christianity recommends the single state, which the Pattern exemplifies. . . . I am unable to comprehend how it can occur to any man to unite being a Christian with being married."[124]

## RESULTS OF MORAL DUALISM

What does the intellectual history of Western culture disclose about prominent attitudes toward human sexuality and their effect upon interpretations of earliest Christianity? First, this survey has shown that sexual asceticism can be traced throughout the course of our civilization. It was advocated by a number of Greek philosophers; it waxed in the Roman and medieval eras; and it has continued with diminishing vigor in modern history. Many important philosophers, in their life-styles and teachings, have denigrated the libidinous. They have assumed that devotion to the life of the immaterial intellect should result in antipathy toward satisfying sensual desires.

The influence of Plato has been especially heavy in this regard. He believed that lovers of wisdom should strive to become disincarnate psyches. Through the mouthpiece of Socrates he asserted:

Genuine philosophers will come to a position such as this: . . . so long as we have the body with us and our soul is mixed up with this evil, we shall not attain satisfactorily our aim of finding truth. For the body is a source of continual trouble. . . . It infects us with loves; desires, fears, all kinds of fancies, and much nonsense, with the result that we lose our intellectual ability. . . . In the present life we come closest to knowledge if we avoid as much as possible all contact or intercourse with the body, and keep ourselves pure from it until God himself shall set us free. In this way, by keeping ourselves uncontaminated by the foolishness of the body, we shall probably reach the company of others like ourselves.

That discussion concludes with the claim that philosophy is a "practice of death" because it provides insight into the fleshless immortal realm.[125]

Nietzsche, after observing that philosophers have had a bent toward scorning sexuality, has aptly suggested why this has been the case. He wrote about some fellow bachelors in this way:

Wherever there have been philosophers, from India to England, there has prevailed a special philosopher's resentment against sensuality. . . . The philosopher abhors marriage, for he sees the married state as an obstacle to fulfillment. What great philosopher has ever been married? Heraclitus, Plato, Descartes, Spinoza, Leibniz, Kant, Schopenhauer—not one of them was married; moreover, it is impossible to imagine any of them married. . . . What, then, does the ascetic ideal betoken in a philosopher? . . . Asceticism provides him with the condition most favorable to the exercise of his intelligence.[126]

A parallel explanation for sexual asceticism in Western philosophy has been given by D. H. Lawrence. With considerable disgust he wrote: "When the great crusade against sex and the body started in full blast with Plato, it was a crusade for 'ideals' and for this 'spiritual' knowledge in apartness."[127] Thus there has been a persistent but perverse tendency among some mainline philosophers to bifurcate the human self into a dishonorable physical part and a noble non-physical faculty. Moreover, they have aspired to become Thomistic angels even before death for they have often aimed at being what Aquinas defined as angel nature, namely "disembodied intellect."[128]

Second, it has been shown that antifeminine bias has been concomitant with moral dualism in Western philosophy. Women were regarded as unworthy of participating in philosophical debate in the Athenian agora. From the classical age onward, philosophical endeavor has been almost exclusively an activity for men. Even though Plato suggested that some women may equal some men's potential for engaging in dialectic, the implications of his radical opinion have generally not been taken seriously. Rather, Aristotle's notion that the masculine cranium is the only fit instrument for profound thought has prevailed. Women are still stereotyped by men as Dionysian rather than Apollonian, intuitive rather than analytical, irrational rather than logical. The result of this gigantic prejudice has probably caused some women of genius as great as men well known in the history of philosophy to live and die unnoticed by the intellectual community. Due more to male chauvinism than to innate ability, there has never been a widely acclaimed female philosopher. Not atypical of philosophers has been Schopenhauer's assessment that women "remain children their whole life long" because they have not been endowed with "a masculine intellect."[129] Because of this assumed natural deficiency women have been usually regarded as basically unfit for philosophical reflection. In the last century philogynist J. S. Mill opposed the traditional assumption of feminine inferiority but misogynist Nietzsche evaluated feminism as the disease of democracy.[130]

Lastly, this study, together with others,[131] suggests that Greek philosophy is a major cause of the sexual asceticism that has infiltrated Christiantity. I have argued elsewhere that this asceticism cannot be accurately traced to earliest Christianity in Palestine.[132] Celibacy in the church sprang not from the nonascetic gospel but from the impact of Hellenism in the postapostolic era. Theologian Emil Brunner has correctly assessed the causal relationship between ancient Greek sexual asceticism and early Christianity.

Through Platonic Hellenistic mysticism the idea penetrated into the early church that the sex element, as such, is something low, and unworthy of intelligent man, an idea which . . . is in absolute opposition to the biblical idea of creation. This idea, actualized in monasticism, erected into a standard in the Catholic ideal of virginity, was not wholly overcome by the Reformation.[133]

Marcion, one of the most notable Christians of the second century, is a case in point. He imposed the stringent requirement of sexual abstinence on his followers. His critics traced his disdainful attitude toward conjugal relations to pagan philosophers. After telling citations from Plato, Clement of Alexandria concluded, "I have shown clearly enough that Marcion took from Plato the starting-point of his strange doctrines."[134] Also Tertullian informs us that Marcion was a "zealous student of Stoicism."[135] As we have seen, Platonism and Stoicism strongly advocated moral dualism.

Marcion was condemned as a heretic, in part because of his stricture against accepting into the church those who were unwilling to renounce sexual relations permanently. Although orthodoxy rejected this extreme form of sexual asceticism, it did perpetuate celibacy for a holier class of Christians. The reason for this practice is expressed in Bishop Ambrose's dictum: "The ministerial office must be kept pure and unspotted, and must not be defiled by coitus."[136] Through the discipline of crushing tender passions it was thought that the divine immortal soul could best be emancipated from its carnal dungeon. In medieval Catholicism moral dualism was the main, though not the exclusive, theoretical basis for the practice of celibacy. Those theologians in church history who have advocated sexual asceticism have often unwittingly held a doctrine of man closer to Athens than to Jerusalem. The self-mortification they have defended stems more from the dialogues of Plato than from the writings of the Bible.

It may not be overly optimistic to hope that a notable accomplishment of our century will be the final elimination of moral dualism and the depreciation of feminine capabilities. Professional philosophers can take little credit for this achievement, for they have in large measure responded to rather than actively initiated this modern trend. Also, there may result from the contemporary sexual revolution a more balanced view of sexuality and a healthier regard for the psychosomatic unity of human personality.

# 5

# The Reformers on Sexuality

ONE of the most abiding contributions of the Protestant Reformation was a deescalation of the medieval crusade against sex. The topics of marriage and celibacy were prominent in the writings of the Reformers of the sixteenth century, who wholeheartedly endorsed marriage for all people—although they had no serious objection to voluntary celibacy for the few with an idiosyncratic preference for it. The principal leaders of the Reformation, Martin Luther, Huldreich Zwingli, and John Calvin, emphasized different reasons for exalting marital sexuality.

## LUTHER'S OUTLOOK

The law prohibiting clerical marriage which had been formulated in medieval Catholicism was denounced by Luther because it was contrary to both biblical custom and natural impulse.[1] With regard to 1 Timothy 4:1-2, which associates the prohibition of marriage with "doctrines of demons," he tersely commented: "Christ wants a minister of the Word to have a wife, but the pope does not. You can see which of them has the spirit of demons." Luther came to believe that celibacy, far from being meritorious, was a liability to chastity. He appealed to the lives of some renowned saints to illustrate that the renunciation of marriage tended more to inflame than suppress desire. Quite specifically this Reformer stated: "When he was quite old Augustine still complained about nocturnal pollutions. When he was goaded by desire Jerome beat his breast with stones but was unable to drive the girl out of his heart. Francis made snowballs and Benedict lay down on thorns."[2] Luther also held that celibates tended to overemphasize sexual sins because they were continually fighting against them with little success. They considered a continent man moral even though he was seething with such major sins as hatred and self-righteousness. This Reformer accurately pointed out that celibates had wrongly equated Paul's exhortation to subdue "the desires of the flesh" with an injunction to avoid lechery.[3]

If Luther's viewpoint is represented by the "table-talk" recorded by one of his disciples, then he assumed that Jesus, unlike the ascetic saints, fully expressed his impulses. Luther held that sexual indulgence between a man and woman who were closely associated was as inevitable as the burning of dry straw when ignited.[4] Since Jesus had feminine companionship on his journeys, Luther believed that he engaged in sexual intercourse.[5]

Luther advocated that followers of Jesus cast aside man-made rules pertaining to coital abstinence and return to the original pattern of creation. Unlike the medieval molders of Christian thought, Luther believed that in Paradise Adam and Eve enjoyed a complete sex life.[6] He maintained that it was not primarily for procreation, but for remedying sexual immorality, that Adam was given a wife. In his commentary on Genesis 2, Luther referred to a wife as medicine; she provides an "antidote against sin." He stated in a letter:

We are all made for marriage, as our bodies show and as the Scriptures state in Gen. 2:18. Whoever, therefore, considers himself a man and believes himself to be included in this general term should hear what God, his Creator, here says and decrees for him. . . . Therefore, whoever will live alone undertakes an impossible task and takes it upon himself to run counter to God's Word and the nature that God has given.[7]

In that letter Luther also forthrightly affirmed that sexual gratification for a human male was as natural and as delectable as eating and drinking. An ancient ditty expresses his outlook: "Who loves not wine, women, and song / Remains a fool his whole life long."[8] Luther, following Paul and Jewish Scripture,[9] insisted that intercourse was a right and a duty for married couples. This famous advice is attributed to Luther: "A week two / Is the woman's due./ Harms neither me nor you, / Makes in a year, twice fifty-two."[10]

Although Luther deviated markedly from the stance of medieval Christianity, he did not discard the sexually ascetic theory of original sin he had assimilated during his years of indoctrination as an Augustinian monk. He agreed with Augustine that sexual desire is inherently sinful and that this wickedness is passed on in human reproduction.[11] Luther asserted:

If Adam had not fallen, the love of bride and groom would have been the loveliest thing. Now this love is not pure either, for each married partner seeks to satisfy his desire with the other, and it is this desire which corrupts marital love. Therefore the married state is no longer pure and free from sin. The temptation of the flesh has become so strong and consuming that marriage may be likened to a hospital for incurables which prevents inmates from falling into graver sin.[12]

This early outlook on marriage became somewhat less myopic after Luther, at the age of forty-two, found a compatible partner. Occasionally he condoned marriage for reasons other than carnal relief or reproduction. "Next to God's Word there is no more precious treasure than holy matrimony. God's highest gift on earth is a pious, cheerful, God-fearing, home-keeping wife, with whom you may live peacefully, to whom you may entrust your goods and body and life."[13] Even so, Luther's main emphasis throughout life was that marriage was a remedy for more heinous sin.[14] In his Augsburg Confession he stated that marriage was instituted "to aid human infirmity and prevent unchastity."[15] His viewpoint on original sin also became a part of early Lutheran doctrine, as this affirmation reveals: "After the fall man received from his parents by heredity a congenitally depraved impulse, filthiness of heart, depraved concupiscences and depraved inclinations."[16]

## ERASMUS AND ZWINGLI

To understand Zwingli's outlook on sexuality it is necessary to explore the writings of Erasmus, for that Dutch scholar was Zwingli's friend and had more influence over him than over any other Reformed leader. Erasmus was an eloquent and constructive protester against medieval celibacy. He was the illegitimate son of a clergyman, so his quip that priests are called "fathers" because of propagation was appropriate. As a youth he experienced the monastic life, but came to believe that chastity was less in danger outside the cloister.

Like others with the Renaissance frame of mind, Erasmus renounced the immediate past and probed ancient sources of Western
civilization for its humanizing content. Nowhere does he better
display this outlook than in his essays on marriage, toward which he
expresses a warmth which shows that he has gone behind the cultural
values of both the medieval and the Greco-Roman eras and has
resurrected the Hebraic outlook. Some of his sentiments on marriage follow.

God said "It is not good for man to be alone," and he created Eve, not out
of mud, as in the case of Adam, but from his rib that none should be closer
and dearer than a wife. . . . Should not marriage be honored above all the
sacraments because it was the first to be instituted, and by God himself? The
other sacraments were established on earth, this one in Paradise; the others
as a remedy, this one as fellowship in felicity. The others were ordained for
fallen nature, but this one for nature unspoiled. . . . The excitation of Venus,
which is necessary for marriage, is from nature and whatever is of nature
is pure and holy. The most holy manner of life, pure and chaste, is marriage.
. . . Moral integrity is nowhere better exemplified than in marriage. . . . I
would like to see permission given to priests and monks to marry, especially
when there is such a horde of priests among whom chastity is rare. . . . I
think that bishops would long since have given this permission if they did
not derive more income from the taxes on concubines than they could reap
from wives. . . . Why refrain from that which God institutes, nature sanctions, reason persuades, divine and human laws approve, the consent of all
nations endorses and to which the highest examples exhort? . . . You are
bound to friends in affection. How much more to a wife in the highest love,
with union of the body, the bond of the sacrament and the sharing of your
goods! . . . Nothing is more safe, felicitous, tranquil, pleasant and lovable
than marriage.[17]

Erasmus' attitude toward sexuality was despised by Catholic official-
dom and consequently his *Encomium of Marriage* was condemned and
burned in 1525.

Zwingli, like his mentor, was aware that the celibacy law of Catholicism had promulgated duplicity in his own country. For example,
a Swiss bishop levied a fine for each child born to a priest. Judging
from the fines collected, there were in 1522 some 1875 babies born
of clerical liaisons![18] Indeed, Zwingli, who had been ordained as a
priest, admitted that he sired at least one bastard. In a letter to a

friend written in 1518, he also confessed that he had been unable to fulfill a vow of continence for longer than one year. He maintained that his conduct should not be considered gross since it was against his principle to seduce a virgin or a nun.[19] After he became pastor of the Great Minster of Zurich he debated this thesis: "I know of no greater scandal than the prohibition of lawful marriage to priests, while they are permitted for money to have concubines. Shame!"[20] In that same year (1523) the city of Zurich made it legal for clergymen to marry. Shortly afterwards he publicly married Anna Reinhard who had been his concubine for two years.[21] Preceding Luther in marriage by one year, Zwingli became the first priest in five centuries to have the audacity to challenge the ecclesiastical law against clerical marriage.

Zwingli's personal experience caused him to believe that the main purpose of marriage was to cure unruly passions.[22] A creed which he helped to formulate at Berne in 1528 states: "Marriage is not forbidden in Scripture to any class of men, but is commanded and permitted to all in order to avoid fornication and unchastity."[23] Whereas Zwingli agreed with Luther that marriage was sanctioned to remedy illicit lust, he departed from the German Reformer's view of congenital depravity. Zwingli rejected the Augustinian doctrine of inherited guilt transmitted from Adam through the semen. Rather he held that original sin refers to a "disease" of self-love that is inherent in human nature.[24]

## CALVIN AND THE PURITANS

Calvin was more optimistic about sex life and more appreciative of women than either the medieval church or Luther had been.[25] Although he defended a grim doctrine of human depravity, like Zwingli he believed that man's tragic fault was arrogant pride—a sin distinct from the libidinous impulse. He judged those medieval churchmen "foolish" who claimed that sensuality was the seat of sin[26] and held that the consummation of sexual desire in marriage could be a holy communion. He was puzzled by the inconsistency of Catholics who "affirm that in the sacrament the grace of the Holy Spirit is conferred; they teach copulation to be a sacrament; and they deny that the Holy Spirit is ever present in copulation."[27]

The purposes of marriage for Calvin were three: companionship, propagation, and a relief for sexual desire. On the basis of the last, and least significant, purpose he reproached Catholic priests in this indignant manner:

Within them there boil unnamable lusts, so that scarce one in ten behaves chastely. And when it comes to the monasteries, plain fornication is the least of all that goes on there. Would their ears open but once to God speaking through the mouth of St. Paul, how they would leap to the remedy which he ordains here; but such is their pride that they turn like tigers on those that would help them to it.[28]

It was by means of scholarly study of the Bible that Calvin arrived at his affirmative position on sexuality. In the Genesis 2 creation account he found that a wife is principally intended to be her husband's "inseparable associate." Calvin asserted that "when marriage is also a remedy for lust we have in it a double gift of God, but the second is incidental." Contained here is a tacit criticism of Luther's and Zwingli's characteristic view of a wife's main role. Those earlier Reformers had thought of her as a safety valve for carnal lust, relieving a man of the urge to behave like a tomcat.

In his Genesis commentary Calvin also spoke of the error of most medieval Christians "who think that woman was formed only for the sake of propagation." Jerome especially irked him, and he asserted that that bishop's polemics were "crammed with petulant insults by which he tries to make sacred marriage hateful and disgraceful." A millenium earlier Jerome had employed flaming rhetoric in urging Christians to "cut down the tree of marriage with the ax of virginity."[29] William Tyndale, like his contemporary Calvin, rebuked the "ungodly persuasions" which Jerome used to promote a "false feigned chastity."[30] For Jerome the only positive purpose of marriage was the production of virgins without which a celibate system could not survive.[31]

It might be said that while the medievalists made Genesis 1:28, "Be fruitful and multiply," the key test pertaining to marriage, Luther and Zwingli made 1 Corinthians 7:9 central—"It is better to marry than to be aflame with passion"—while Calvin made Genesis 2:18, "It is not good for man to be alone," the basic authority.

Elsewhere in his interpretation of the Pentateuch Calvin underlined the positive Hebraic outlook on sexual relations within marriage. The provision for exemption from military service in Deuteronomy 24:5, so that a man can "cheer" his bride, elicited this comment: "The immunity here given has for its object the awakening of the mutual love which may preserve the conjugal fidelity of husband and wife. . . . That God should permit a bride to enjoy herself with her husband affords no trifling proof of his indulgence."

The Geneva Reformer discovered that even the apostle Paul championed frequent coital encounters between married couples. In his exposition of 1 Corinthian 7 Calvin wrote: "Conjugal intercourse is a thing that is pure, honorable and holy, because it is a pure institution of God." He perceptively summarized the argument of that chapter in this way:

As far as we can gather from what Paul says, the Corinthians had become strongly influenced by the supersititious notion that virginity is an outstanding, almost an angelic virtue, so that they despised marriage as if it were something unclean. In order to get rid of this mistaken view, Paul teaches that each individual must know what his particular gift is; and in this connection must not try to do something he has not got the ability to do; for everybody is not called to the same state.[32]

Two other comments by Calvin in his commentary on 1 Corinthians express vividly the Reformer's outlook on women and sexuality. With regard to 1 Corinthians 7, a chapter that has often been used by celibates to denigrate marriage, Calvin wrote:

No room is allowed for the vulgar jokes, which are generally made in order to discredit marriage, such as, "a wife is a necessary evil," and "a woman is one of the greatest of evils." For sayings like that have come from Satan's laboratory; and their objective is nothing less than the branding of God's holy institution as dishonorable, so that, as a consequence, men may shrink from marriage, as though from the gallows and plague.

In 1 Corinthians 9:5 Paul wrote: "Have I no right to take a Christian wife about with me, like the rest of the apostles and the Lord's brothers, and Cephas?" On that verse Calvin sarcastically but accurately noted:

It was later than the apostles that men lit upon the remarkable piece of wisdom that the priests of the Lord are defiled if they have intercourse with their lawful wives. At last it went so far that Pope Syricus had no hesitation about calling marriage "an uncleanness of the flesh, in which no one can please God." What, then, will happen to the unfortunate apostles, who persisted in this impurity until their death?

After looking at Calvin's relatively positive view of marital sexuality, it appears at first glance incongruous that he, like the other Reformers, refused to call marriage a sacrament. The difficulty here is due to the ambiguity of the term *sacrament,* which could mean a mutual pledge, a symbol of something divine, or a ceremony instituted by Jesus for the church. In the late Middle Ages the latter meaning was dominant, for the church found it could aggrandize its power by claiming that the faithful should be infused with grace administered by clerics. The Reformers found no biblical warrant for considering marriage a distinctive Christian rite. They realized that the divine blessing was bestowed upon all married couples, be they pagan or Christian, from the creation of marriage.[33] Paradoxically, the Reformers did not reject marriage as a sacrament because they thought it was less sacred an institution than their Catholic opponents. On the contrary, they saw that the church had no authority to add to or subtract from its holiness.

Calvin's personal experience, as well as his biblical outlook, explains his position on marriage. During the decade that he was married the child he fathered died in infancy. It was probably in part because of that experience and because of his appreciation of his wife's partnership that he saw excellence in marriage apart from producing progeny. After her death he wrote: "I have been bereaved of the best companion of my life, who, if our lot had been harsher, would have been not only the willing sharer of exile and poverty, but even of death. While she lived she was the faithful helper of my ministry."[34]

Calvin, the father of Puritanism, contributed significantly to the outlook on sex and marriage in the Puritan tradition. Although there is the ignorant popular assumption that the Puritans were sexual ascetics, that was certainly not the outlook of classical Puritanism. Literary critic R. M. Frye states: "Early Puritanism consciously taught the purity, legality, and even obligation of physical love in marriage."[35] R. V. Schnucker, in a recent dissertation on Puritan writings prior to 1630 concludes that the Puritans vigorously defended marital coitus as necessary and wholesome.[36] They consciously attempted to return to the biblical belief in the basic goodness of conjugal relations.

John Milton, the most illustrious figure of English Puritanism, extolled ardent connubial love as a great good. Consciously following the Geneva Reformer of the previous century, he acknowledged that the prime reason why marriage is ordained for man is "to comfort and refresh him against the evil of solitary life."[37] Milton recognized that loneliness is the first thing in Scripture which God calls not good. He fully endorsed the implication which Calvin drew from the story of Adam becoming "one flesh" with Eve: "It will follow that the children of God may embrace a conjugal life with a good and tranquil conscience, and husbands and wives may live together in chastity and honor."[38]

In *Paradise Lost,* sex in marriage is a virtue of the ideal state and is hailed as "the crown of all our bliss." The Puritan bard expressed his sentiments in this interpretation of the Garden of Eden story:

> Into their inmost bower
> Handed they went; and, eased the putting off
> These troublesome disguises which we wear,
> Straight side by side were laid, nor turned, I ween,
> Adam from his fair spouse; nor Eve the rites
> Mysterious of connubial love refused. . . .
> These lulled by nightingales, embracing slept,
> And on their naked limbs the flowery roof
> Showered roses, which the morn repaired. Sleep on
> Blest pair; and O yet happiest if ye seek
> No happier state, and know to know no more.[39]

Quite contrary to the imaginings of ascetic church fathers, Milton's Satan tries to disrupt marital love by advocating abstinence.[40] Accordingly Milton ridiculed those who stigmatized connubial sexuality.

> Hypocrites austerely talk
> Of purity and place and innocence,
> Defaming as impure what God declares
> Pure, and commands to some, leaves free to all.[41]

One of the outstanding Calvinists of the past century is Charles
Hodge. His treatment of marriage summarizes the position on that
subject of a main Protestant tradition. It is thoroughly biblical and
deserves to be quoted at length:

The very fact that God created man, male and female, delaring that it was
not good for either to be alone, and constituted marriage in Paradise, should
be decisive on this subject. The doctrine which degrades marriage by making it a less holy state, has its foundation in Manicheism or Gnosticism. It
assumes that evil is essentially connected with matter; that sin has its seat and
source in the body; that holiness is attainable only through asceticism and
neglecting the body; that because the "vita angelica" is a higher form of life
than that of men here on earth, therefore marriage is a degradation. . . . Our
Lord more than once quotes and enforces the original law given in Gen.
2:24, that a man shall "leave his father and his mother, and shall cleave unto
his wife, and they shall be one flesh." The same passage is quoted by the
Apostle as containing a great and symbolic truth (Eph. 5:31). It is thus
taught that the marriage relation is the most intimate and sacred that can
exist on earth, to which all other human relations must be sacrified. We
accordingly find that from the beginning, with rare exceptions, patriarchs,
prophets, apostles, confessors, and martyrs, have been married men. . . .
There has been no more prolific source of evil to the church than the
unscriptural notion of the special virtue of virginity.[42]

It is possible to go through the writings of Luther, Zwingli, Calvin, and their followers and point out ways in which their outlooks
on sex and marriage are far less than ideal. In this regard Paul Tillich
has made a balanced judgment: "The suspicion of libido was so
deeply rooted in the Christian tradition that . . . the Reformers were
unable to eradicate the remnants of Neo-Platonic asceticism, and
were suspicious of everything sexual. . . . The Reformers tried to
re-establish the dignity of the sexual, but they succeeded only in a
limited way."[43] However, compared to their time and perhaps even
compared to our time they had a more holistic viewpoint than their
critics. Calvin's stress upon the companionship motive for marriage
was especially important for it encouraged many Christians to break
out of the medieval straitjacket on sexuality and resurrect the best
of the apostolic perspective that husband and wife are "joint heirs
of the grace of life."[44]

# 6

# *William Blake on Joseph's Dilemma*

Two centuries ago the ecentric English mystic, William Blake, created poetry and paintings that contain profound theology. In recent years a number of fresh probes into his original religious thought have been made.[1] However, appreciation of Blake has not been extended to include his supposition that Jesus was conceived by means of an illicit union. Indeed, some respond to the notion that Joseph's betrothed may not have been chaste with a contempt not unlike that of Simon the Pharisee. He was convinced that Jesus could not be a spokesman for God because he accepted a "woman of the city who was a sinner."[2]

Blake's outlook on Joseph and Mary may be more in harmony with Jesus' gospel than his critics care to acknowledge. With respect to the purpose of the incarnation, he championed a traditional doctrine of the church. His affirmation, "God becomes as we are that we may be as he is,"[3] is essentially a restatement of the position of some patristic molders of orthodoxy. In the second century Bishop Irenaeus wrote: "He who was the son of God became the son of man, that man . . . might become the son of God."[4] The Nicene theologian Athanasius likewise declared that the Logos "became human that we might be made divine."[5]

## MARY'S PREGNANCY

It is Blake's unconventional interpretation of the mode of the incarnation that is repugnant to traditional Christians. Believing that stories of virgin conceptions wrongly emphasize the sanctity of sexual abstinence, he rejected the canonized accounts of Mary's conceiving miraculously without physical insemination. How then, according to Blake, was Mary's first pregnancy accomplished? He assumes on the basis of a portion of the Matthean nativity story that Joseph had not fathered her baby. There Blake read: "Now the birth of Jesus Christ was on this wise: When as his mother Mary was espoused to Joseph, before they came together, she was found with child of the Holy Ghost. Then Joseph her husband, being a just man, and not willing to make her a public example, was minded to put her away privily."[6] Those verses prompted Blake to raise a historical and moral question in the context of a Christological declaration:

> Was Jesus Born of a Virgin Pure,
> With narrow Soul and looks demure?
> If he intended to take on Sin
> The Mother should an Harlot been,
> Just such a one as Magdalen
> With seven devils in her Pen.[7]

Is there any basis for Blake's speculation concerning Jesus' mother? Proof of paternity is notably difficult, if not impossible, to establish. However, if Joseph was not the physical father of Jesus, and if human sperm is a necessity for fertilization, then Blake is not bizarre in suggesting that Mary's first child was sired by a paramour.

There are indications in the Gospels that some living in the first Christian century may have believed that Mary was unfaithful to her betrothed. The Matthean genealogy involves some prominent illicit unions of Hebrew history, and the compiler may have thought they established a precedent for Mary's pregnancy.[8] Though the mention of any women in such listings was unusual in ancient Jewish records, Matthew 1:1–16 contains the names of several who became mothers in irregular ways. The first, Tamar, was impregnated by Judah, who took her to be a harlot. Next, Matthew claims that Rahab, a notorious prostitute, was an ancestress of Jewish royalty. In the genealogy which immediately precedes the story of Mary's conception, reference is also made to Bathsheba, with whom David committed adultery.[9] It was significant to Blake that these scandalous women were part of Jesus' family tree.[10]

There are other New Testament and extrabiblical shreds of evidence which may suggest that Mary conceived Jesus in the course of a liaison. According to John 8:41, Jesus' adversaries say: "We were not born of fornication." This may possibly show that some Jewish opponents of early Christianity insinuated that Jesus was born of an illicit union.[11] From at least as early as the medieval era such a tradition has been alive in Judaism.[12] Also, this charge was accepted by some pagans: "The mother of Jesus was turned out by the carpenter who was betrothed to her, as she had been convicted of adultery and had a child by a certain soldier named Panthera."[13] Similarly, Tertullian in the second century alludes to a Roman joke about Jesus being the son of a whore.[14]

Blake was not a learned man, but he was interested in the study of the original Hebrew and Greek sources of Christianity,[15] and consequently may have been aware of those accusations regarding Jesus' paternity. He jars Christian piety by not dismissing them as untrue and foul blasphemy. Rather, he seemed to think that the significance of the gospel is enhanced if Jesus was conceived in an affair involving a breach of the Decalogue. Blake envisaged Mary as a forerunner of her son who rejected Mosaic legalism. Jesus is portrayed as an antinomian who "mock'd the Sabbath" and discarded Moses' curses against the "impure."[16]

Blake held that Christian expositors have tried to gloss over the revolutionary sexual ethic of Jesus. Northrop Frye expresses well the iconoclastic perspective of Blake: "The Bible must be shaken upside-down before it will yield all its secrets. The priests have censored and clipped and mangled: they give us a celibate Jesus born of a virgin without the slightest 'stain' of sexual contact, which is blasphemous nonsense."[17]

### JOSEPH'S FORGIVENESS

In *Jerusalem,* an epic poem written by Blake in the latter part of his career, a daring attempt is made to reconstruct the dilemma Joseph faced on realizing that his betrothed had become pregnant by someone else. If Joseph called public attention to Mary's unfaithfulness, his townspeople might carry out the Mosaic law and gruesomely stone her to death.[18] But if he chose to accept the child of Mary as his own, he would fail to dispense the retributive justice which was expected of a self-respecting and righteous Jew. And so this agonizing dialogue ensues:

Mary said, "If thou put me away from thee
Dost thou not murder me?" Joseph spoke in anger and fury, "Should I
Marry a Harlot and an Adulteress?" Mary answer'd, "Art thou more pure
Than thy Maker who forgiveth Sins and calls again Her that is Lost?
Tho' She hates, he calls her again in love. I love my dear Joseph,
But he driveth me away from his presence; yet I hear the voice of God
In the voice of my husband: tho' he is angry for a moment, he will not
Utterly cast me away; if I were pure, never could I taste the sweets
Of the Forgiveness of Sins; if I were holy, I could never behold the tears
Of love of him who loves me in the midst of his anger in furnace of fire."
"Ah, my Mary!" said Joseph, weeping over and embracing her closely in
His arms. . . ."I heard his voice in my sleep and his Angel in my dream,
Saying, . . . If you Forgive one another, so shall Jehovah Forgive you,
That He Himself may Dwell among You. Fear not then to take
To thee Mary thy Wife, for she is with Child by the Holy Ghost."
Then Mary burst forth into a Song.[19]

In this bold interpretation of Matthew 1:18–20, Blake displays how humans should resolve ambivalent impulses of revenge and compassion by reflecting on God's love. The episode clarifies what Blake took to be the essence of true religion: "This alone is the Gospel and this is the Life and Immortality brought to light by Jesus. Even the Covenant of Jehovah, which is This: If you forgive one another your Trespasses, so shall Jehovah forgive you. That he himself may dwell among you; but if you Avenge, you Murder the Divine Image, and he cannot dwell among you."[20]

Blake was repelled by the "pale Virgin shrouded in snow"[21] who has commonly been adored by Christians as the paragon of virtue. He believed that the doctrine of the virginal conception of Jesus erroneously stressed an intact hymen and the absence of libidinous passion as the basis of purity in the holy family. Far from seeing virtue in perpetual virginity, Blake deemed it sinful to abase one's sexual desires. The "Religion of Chastity," he claimed, "clos'd up in Moral Pride" the "Head and Heart and Loins."[22] To those who associated the religion of Jesus with sensuous renunciation, Blake retorted:

> The Vision of Christ that thou dost see
> Is my Vision's Greatest Enemy. . . .
> Thy Heaven doors are my Hell gates.[23]

In his epic poem Blake called attention to Joseph, a figure long neglected by theologians. He believed that the Gospel is truncated by the orthodox legend of an aloof protector, an immaculate lady, and her sexless son. Rather, it can best be expressed in the story of a forgiving husband, a repentant adulteress, and a son with similar traits of character. The mutual reconciliation of Joseph and Mary becomes the epiphany of God-with-us, Emmanuel. That interpersonal resolution of hostilities, rather than parthenogenetic violation of natural human generation, becomes the centerpeice of the Christmas story. If there is a miracle in the nativity drama, it is Joseph's compassionate acceptance of his prodigal wife and her child. Blake exclaims:

> O holy Generation, Image of Regeneration!
> O point of mutual forgiveness between Enemies!
> Birthplace of the Lamb of God incomprehensible![24]

Blake's perspective on sexuality can be related to a New Testament proverb: "To the pure all things are pure."[25] Holiness is associated with a cleansed internal attitude rather than with an untampered physical condition. In spite of Mary's irregular means of conception, she and her baby are holy because of her genuine love for the man she had wronged. J. Middleton Murry comments on Blake's unique interpretation of the Incarnation in this way: "Mary is with child by the Holy Ghost, because the babe in her womb is lifted to Eternity by the act of Forgiveness."[26]

## "THE EVERLASTING GOSPEL"

It is intriguing to muse on the effect that a profound parental alienation-forgiveness experience could have had on Jesus. Realizing that much of a child's theology is communicated to him by the quality of relations within his home, can it be that Jesus' rejection of revenge was in part due to the influence of Joseph? When Jesus taught, "Be merciful, even as your Father is merciful,"[27] could he have had in mind as a model the father who reared him in Nazareth? Jesus' favorite designation for God, "Daddy,"[28] was probably affected by his admiration of the character qualities of Joseph. Moreover, his appreciation of his parents' love may well have contributed to his favoring repentant outcasts more than self-righteous prigs. He shocked the latter by asserting: "I did not come to call the virtuous, but sinners"; and "the tax collectors and the harlots go into the kingdom of God before you."[29]

The similarity of temperament between Blake's Jesus and Joseph may be discerned in lines of *The Everlasting Gospel* that follow:

> The morning blush'd fiery red:
> Mary was found in Adulterous bed;
> Earth groan'd beneath, and Heaven above
> Trembled at discovery of Love
> Jesus was sitting in Moses' Chair,
> They brough the trembling Woman There.
> Moses commands she be stoned to death,
> What was the sound of Jesus' breath?. . .
> "Mary, Fear Not! Let me see
> The Seven Devils that torment thee:
> Hide not from my Sight thy Sin,
> That forgiveness thou maist win". . . .
> The Publicans and Harlots he
> Selected for his Company,
> And from the Adulteress turn'd away
> God's righteous Law, that lost its Prey.[30]

The unnamed adulterous woman of John 8:2–11 is identified in that poem with Mary Magdalene. Since she was a companion of Jesus during his travels, Blake asks: "Was Jesus Chaste?" and implies that the query should be answered in the negative. Whether Jesus was celibate or not, Blake endorsed the New Testament declaration that Jesus "was tempted in every respect as we are."[31]

> What was it which he took on
> That he might bring Salvation?
> A Body subject to be Tempted,
> From neither pain nor grief Exempted?
> Or such a body as might feel
> The passions that with Sinners deal?[32]

Blake's genius in biblical interpretation is further discerned in the way he relates the compassion of Joseph and Jesus for adulterers to the God of prophetic Judaism. In *Jerusalem,* after telling of Joseph's act of forgiveness, the poet shows how steadfast love in spite of unfaithfulness epitomized the "covenant of Jehovah" prior to the coming of Christianity. He affirms that it was through experiences of infidelity that Jerusalem came to the realization that God's restoration was free—"without money and without price." She testifies: "If I were unpolluted I should never have Glorified Thy Holiness, or rejoiced in thy great Salvation."[33] Several of the prophetic books may have been the source of Blake's personification of Israel as a harlot. Hosea called his nation a wanton mother, but promised that after she repented her children would be called "the sons of the Living God."[34] The prophet's imagery may have been stimulated by his personal experience with Gomer, his unfaithful wife—an experience not dissimilar to the dilemma of Blake's Joseph. Hosea believed that God had commanded him to "love a woman who is beloved of a paramour and is an adulteress, even as the Lord loves the people of Israel."[35] Ezekiel articulated God's brokenheartedness over his precious bride Jerusalem, who brazenly prostituted herself to foreign lovers, and told of the divine forgiveness awaiting her return to him.[36] Isaiah also employed the metaphor of God as a husband of Judah. After that wife's shameful conduct, her Spouse says: "In sudden anger for a moment I hid my face from you; but with everlasting love I will have compassion on you."[37] Thus the Blakean treatment of God's "marriage" with wayward Israel is based on a prominent motif in the Old Testament.

Blake comprehended that the basic teaching of the entire Bible was that love should be displayed without ceasing to the undeserving. He thought this love could be most poignantly tested in a situation of estrangement provoked by an adulterous conception. Blake's Joseph renewed his trust in one who pleaded for forgiveness after she had betrayed his confidence. Far from believing that his betrothed was forever tainted by past indulgence in illicit coitus, he accepted her child as his own. The couple mutually witnesses to the unfailing nature of true love.

The interpretations of the sexual dilemmas of Joseph and Jesus by Blake are saturated with a major theme of biblical theology. He shows that Jesus was related to Joseph in spirit even if not in flesh, and that Joseph could have been a cuckold without the Incarnation being thereby denigrated. As Rahab is acknowledged as a heroine of "faith" in the New Testament, so Mary can be called "blessed."[38] Even as Leonardo Da Vinci is a great man, albeit a bastard, so Jesus can be acclaimed the God-man regardless of his physical mode of generation. If anything Blake's treatment of the interpersonal relationship between Joseph and Mary adds grandeur to the divine enfleshment and enables us to behold the grace of God in a piquant way.

Attractive though Blake's poetry is, the historical probability that Jesus was procreated by Joseph and his betrothed is at least as great as the assumption that Mary conceived illicitly. After thorough research Rabbi Joseph Klausner argues that Joseph was Jesus' father and that the Jewish charge that Jesus was a bastard was a calumny invented to counter the claim of some Christians that Jesus was virginally conceived.[39] The story of Joseph's dilemma may originally have been a figurative way of expressing the Hebraic concept of dual paternity. As we have seen, the Hebrews assumed that womb fertilization is effected by both the Spirit of God and the sperm of man.

# 7

# *D. H. Lawrence's Appraisal of Jesus*

DURING this last third of the twentieth century Christian appreciation is growing for D. H. Lawrence, a gifted English writer of the century's first third. Bishop J. A. T. Robinson rescued Lawrence from the ranks of literary pornographers at a celebrated legal hearing in 1960 pertaining to the ban on circulation of *Lady Chatterley's Lover.* He showed that adulterous sexual communion could be for Lawrence an unadulterated holy communion.[1] In his controversial *Honest to God,* the Anglican Bishop held that Lawrence's insights on personal relationships were close to his own.[2] More recently, church historian Horton Davies has defended Lawrence as a Christian, although heretical, who was trying to remove smut and shame from sexuality.[3] In the study that follows an investigation will be made of what Lawrence regarded as of primary significance in Jesus or in any other model of morality—namely, the quality of his emotional reciprocation.

## "THE ESCAPED COCK"

Lawrence forthrightly expressed his outlook on Jesus in a work which he entitled *The Escaped Cock.* This short novel, his last important work of fiction, has been published since his death in 1930 under the less virile title, *The Man Who Died.* "The man" is not named in the book but it is apparent that the author had Jesus in mind. To Lawrence, the Christian's paradigm of manhood was defective and revolting. He pictured Jesus as an emotionally anemic being who never desired a sexual companion. That pallid Palestinian was unable to fathom the redemptive love found among those who value mutual sharing. Like Lady Chatterley's impotent husband, Lawrence's

Jesus was inert from the waist down. "Touch me not!" was the frigid prophet's motto. In that novel we are shown true love as being completely distorted by that self-abnegating healer and teacher, disdainful of anyone who might attempt to break his perfect record of altruism.

Only after Jesus' public ministry was over did he realize the error of being totally outgiving. He confessed that the career which ended with the crucifixion was marked by the "greed of giving." Life lacked moderation: "I gave more than I took, and that also is woe and vanity."[4] He lamented that he had asked his disciples to "love with dead bodies."[5] After the revival of his former "dead" flesh, he came to see that the virginal life, far from being pure and virtuous, was "a form of greed."[6] Lawrence suggests that those engaged in life styles of sexual deprivation are selfishly attempting to protect themselves from the risks of physical involvement.

Jesus' outlook on sex, as Lawrence presents it, was the end result of an ugly moral dualism that began with Greek philosphy. The novelist has Lady Chatterley say, "The human body is only coming to real life. With the Greeks it gave a lovely flicker, then Plato and Aristotle killed it, and Jesus finished it off. But now the body is coming really to life, it is really rising from the tomb."[7]

In *The Escaped Cock* Lawrence not only scathingly denounces the quality of love he ascribes to Jesus but audaciously goes on to suggest how he should have lived. Lawrence believed that the ideal man is responsive to the beauty of the sensate realm. Consequently he told of Jesus' victorious struggle to reconcile his instinctive sexual impulse with his spirituality in a reanimated existence. But Lawrence was only incidentally interested in the historical Jesus. His real focus in the novel was on the modern Christian who participates in Jesus' tragi-triumphant drama. Lawrence was influenced by Paul's mysticism: "If we have become one with him by sharing his death, we shall also be one with him by sharing his resurrection."[8] In a parallel manner Lawrence testified: "It is time for the Lord in us to arise. . . . Men in the tomb rise up, the time is expired. The Lord is risen. Quick! Let us follow him."[9]

As a way of showing us the full man, be he the Pauline second Adam or current man, Lawrence employed the literary device of writing an imaginary conclusion for Jesus' life. Though left for dead,

Lawrence's Jesus revives without supernatural assistance. Like a cock at dawn, Jesus becomes rejuvenated at Easter for a new day. Overcome by a "nausea of utter disillusion" with his former life and eager to escape from Magdalene who, in imitation of her Savior, gives without taking, he flees to Sidon on the lovely Lebanese coast, where he finds a place to sleep on the precincts of a temple of Isis. There, attending the bereaved goddess, is a young, unsullied priestess. Identifying herself with Isis' aspiration, the virgin has waited in anguish for the fragments of dead Osiris to be brought together and resurrected. For years she has sought the mystic ecstasy which, she believed, would envelope her when she could "fold her arms round the reassembled body till it became warm again, and roused to life, and could embrace her, and could fecundate her womb."[10] She had passed up the opportunity to serve Caesar as mistress because she found him too rapacious to arouse her. Only when she encountered Jesus did she find fulfillment of her spiritual and physical quest. She adored him because he was, for her, the resurrected Osiris. Her passion for Jesus is described in this way: "She felt it in the quick of her soul. And her agitation was intense."[11]

Jesus likewise had lived the deficient life of a solitary celibate and had championed selfless love. Now he discovers that give-and-take affection among humans is more liberating than the give-and-give ethic he formerly taught and practiced. The gracious words and actions of the priestess cause a sensual desire to swell up in his loins for the first time. Reluctant to become vulnerable, he asks in fear and trembling, "Dare I come into this tender touch of life."[12] But he yields, and "there dawned on him the reality of the soft warm love which is in touch, and which is full of delight." As the priestess massages his wounds, he exclaims: "I am going to be whole! . . . I shall be a man!"[13] Jesus is now titillated with a passion quite different from his passion at Calvary.

Stooping, he laid his hand softly on her warm, bright shoulder, and the shock of desire went through him. . . . He crouched to her, and he felt the blaze of his manhood and his power rise up in his loins, magnificent. "I am risen!". . . He untied the string of linen tunic, and slipped the garment down, till he saw the white glow of her white-gold breasts. And he touched them and he felt his life go molten. "Father!" he said, "why did you hide this from me?" And he touched her with the poignancy of wonder, and the marvellous piercing transcendence of desire. "Lo!" he said, "this is beyond prayer." . . . So he knew her, and was one with her.[14]

The Christian doctrine of Jesus' bodily resurrection provided Lawrence with symbolism for this climatic scene in his short novel: he portrayed Jesus as risen in the whole of his flesh—including his genitals. Lawrence expanded on this theme in his essay "The Risen Lord":

If Jesus rose as a full man, in full flesh and soul, then He rose to take a woman to Himself, to live with her, and to know the tenderness and blossoming of the twoness with her. . . . If Jesus rose in the full flesh, He rose to know the tenderness of a woman, and the great pleasure of her, and to have children by her. He rose to know the responsibility and the peculiar delight of children, and also the exasperation and the nuisance of them.[15]

In his imaginative novella Lawrence was not attempting to correct the church's understanding of Jesus' postmortem life. Rather, he was vigorously asserting that an exemplar of true humanity cannot be thought of as an asexual being who never had an erection.

## THE SENSUOUS JESUS

But was, in fact, the historical Jesus aloof from sexual impulses and conjugal relations? It now appears that Lawrence, like most other Christians, was unable to read the Gospels except through the blurring lenses of ascetic eisegetes. However, the life-style of Jesus "in the days of his flesh" was a complementary self-giving and self-fulfillment. Through "losing his life" in devotion to others, there were some gratifications which he received in return, both intangible and tangible. He was affectionate toward women who anointed his body and who itinerated with him. The words of Jesus to Magdalene in *Superstar* harmonize with the historical record. Her comforting song and caresses evoke this response: "That feels nice . . . She alone has tried to give me what I need right here and now."[16]

Dorothea Krook has aptly criticized Lawrence's portrait of Jesus in this terse comment: "If ever a man was in touch with the phenomenal world and never lost touch with it, that man was Jesus."[17] Both figuratively and literally Jesus was in touch with the sensate world. In his parables he used the connubial life to illustrate the optimum life. When criticized for rejecting the funereal aspects of traditional piety, Jesus compared the religious life to the gaiety of a wedding party.[18] In this respect Jesus and Lawrence both championed a life-affirming philosophy. Davies comments: "Lawrence believed that life should be a marriage feast celebrated with great joy and dancing."[19] Jesus did not attempt to sever spiritual blossoms from carnal roots by believing that the heavenly-minded person would be contaminated by delightful earthy relationships. Rather, he held that man should not put asunder the spiritual carnality that God had joined together.

Lawrence might well have found the original Jesus acceptable. Ralph Sturm plausibly conjectures:

It seems safe to say that he probably would not have rejected the Christ of the Gospel as he was understood in apostolic times. . . .The Christ of whom Lawrence spoke was always inevitably a Christ colored by the face of twentieth-century Christianity, a Christ partially consisting of Puritan rigidity, spiritualism, and angelism. The Christ Lawrence rejected was a kind of ethereal non-human Christ.[20]

Had Lawrence been able to de-Hellenize Christianity and see Jesus as a member of the culture which treasured the sensuous Song of Solomon, he probably would not have censured Jesus. Later in the century in which Jesus lived, the distinguished Rabbi Akiba called that Song the holiest part of the sacred writings.[21] The Hebrew Bible uses the same verb, *aheb*, for both the spiritual and physical facets of love relation. In the Song of Solomon *aheb* refers to the craving mutually felt by bride and bridegroom. In an analogical manner the verb is frequently used elsewhere in the Scriptures to describe the reciprocal devotion between God and his people.

In the Septuagint, the Bible of early Christianity, *aheb* is usually translated by *agapan*. That Greek verb and its substantive form, *agape*, became the key concept of the New Testament. Its writers use *agapan* and its derivatives to designate various kinds of love relationship: between God and man or between man and his fellow man;[22] that which Jesus received from and gave to some women;[23] and that between a devoted husband and wife.[24] Thus *agapan* points to both the physical and spiritual dimensions of love.

### THE HOLISTIC LIFE

It would seem that Jesus and his fellow Jews succeeded better than Lawrence in commitment to the holistic life. They did not elevate sex to a transcendent ultimate, and they realized that full human vitality demanded more than genital satisfaction. But neither did they denigrate sexual intercourse and look upon it as merely an animal act. Indeed, in ancient Judaism sex was accepted as a God-given means for enhancing the companionship and procreative purpose of marriage. As a Jewish male, Jesus came from a culture that regarded marital sexuality as a holy communion.

Lawrence sought in all his writings to describe the balanced life. Only when the emotions and the mind were given their just due, he believed, could personality come into full bloom. But he was not successful. In reaction to the flesh-abhorring Victorian society of his youth, he was preoccupied with the carnal side of the love relationship. To those of his culture who claimed that sex is sin he overreacted by insisting that sensuality is salvation. As Dean Peerman perceptively writes: "Lawrence is to be held responsible not for salaciously cheapening sex, but the opposite—for magnifying its meaning, for overvaluing it to the point of idolatrous glorification, for according it saving power."[25]

In some of his writings Lawrence seems to be unwittingly dualistic. Occasionally he separates the physiological from the psychological aspects of love. A two-tiered theory of personality, in which the cerebral and the tactile are sharply differentiated, is set forth in his creed: "My great religion is belief in the blood, the flesh, as being wiser than the intellect. We can go wrong in our minds. But what our flesh believes and says, is always true."[26] This commitment suggests that Lawrence may have more in common with the phallic cults than with biblical religion. In the former momentary passion and fertile nature are exalted; in the latter the action of God is celebrated in the brain as well as in the viscera. Man and woman do not live by rolls of bread or by rolls in bed alone. The "life which is life indeed" cannot be equated with a satisfactory functioning of the flesh.

Lawrence is deficient in his constructive efforts even though his attack on sexual prudery and obscenity is commendable. On this point William Hoyt's analogy is appropriate.

While Lawrence can diagnose the ills of sick relationships, he does not provide much help in developing a model for healthier ones. . . . Indeed Lawrence seems to have known less, not more, than is contained in the best of Christian tradition about warmth and commitment and wholeness within the marital relationship, including the sexual aspects of that relation. . . . Growing up in the Victorian era . . . Lawrence understandably stumped for the physical to the extent of virtually denying the transcendent in man's life. But since he presents an unbalanced view of man, his work can be no more than a corrective.[27]

Hoyt's criticism, although somewhat excessive, is especially germane to Lawrence's exaltation of temporary affairs in *The Escaped Cock* and in *Lady Chatterley's Lover*. In both works the couples who indulge in coitus are not responsibly concerned about the children they generate. *The Escaped Cock* concludes with the picture of a satiated man sailing away from his pregnant consort. That man may represent the fickle Pan of Hellenistic escapades, but not the faithful Lord of Hebrew history.

On the positive side, a significant contribution of Lawrence is his insistence that mature love should not be viewed as a unilateral altruism. A touch-me-not attitude toward one's body, he held, is vicious; for life is desecrated when tender feelings are not accorded at least as much dignity as dispassionate reason. Lawrence was convinced that physical intimacy should be regarded as a divinely given way of rising above egoistic impulses. Human relations at their best involve a dynamic and delightful giving and receiving between individuals.

In recognizing the potential unselfishness of sexuality, Lawrence parts company not only with the Augustinian Christians but also with the Freudian naturalist. Freud's theory that the libido functions primarily to gratify the individual's "pleasure principle" implies that other persons are normally used as instruments of self-centered satisfaction.[28] Latter-day Augustinians have been delighted with Freud because that atheist seems to provide objective confirmation of their doctrine of congenital depravity. Man's sexual drive, as interpreted by Freud, has been used to prove that by physical heredity humans have a lifelong tendency to take without giving.

Lawrence's view has been reinforced by the clinical discoveries of some psychoanalysts who are currently influential. W. R. D. Fairbairn counters Freud's view of the sexual drive by maintaining that the goal of the libido changes in normal human development. As a person attains maturity the predominately "taking" aim is replaced by a "giving" aim. Man's basic aim, according to Fairbairn, is to attain and cultivate interpersonal relationships. The individual who aims at satiating sexual appetites to the deprivation of others has been distorted by previously unsatisfactory personal relations.[29] In support of this outlook Erich Fromm has written: "The culmination of the male sexual function lies in the act of giving; the man gives himself, his sexual organ, to the woman. . . . She gives herself too; she opens the gates to her feminine center. . . . If she can only receive, she is frigid."[30]

In an apologia written late in life Lawrence stated that his efforts were directed at bringing together "love in all its manifestations, from genuine desire to tender love, love of our fellow men, and love of God."[31] He protested against a type of counterfeit Christianity that views man essentially as a bodiless soul. He abhorred the perspective of those who see life in the flesh as something to be endured rather than enjoyed, a grim existence awaiting the day when the worthless physical husk will be discarded. To counter that life-style Lawrence used the shock tactic of providing an alternative ending to the gospel. By means of *The Escaped Cock* he has helped to exorcise the Gnostic ghost that perennially haunts the figure of Jesus. He has rightly repudiated the Christianity that, by overemphasizing Jesus' bloody death to the negation of his red-blooded life, has concern with "only half of the Passion."[32]

# 8

## *Kazantzakis on Jesus' Sexuality*

THROUGHOUT his life Nikos Kazantzakis (1883–1957) was fascinated by Jesus and the Christian saints. That most widely translated of modern Greek writers thought of Jesus as a supreme type of human suffering from suppressed sensual desires. Consequently, the agonizing Christ figure was prominent in most of his writings in a latent if not in a manifest way. In the prologue to one of his last novels, *The Last Temptation of Christ,* Kazantzakis claimed that "Christ passed through all the stages which the man who struggles passes through. . . . If he had not within him this warm human element, he would never be able to touch our hearts with such assurance and tenderness; he would not be able to become a model for our lives."[1]

Kazantzakis was eager to rescue his paradigm of morality from the insipid Jesus of the hagiographers. In a letter written after completing *The Last Temptation* the purpose of the book is disclosed.

It's a laborious, sacred, creative endeavor to reincarnate the essence of Christ, setting aside the dross-falsehoods and pettiness which all the churches and all the cassocked representatives of Christianity have heaped upon his figure, thereby distorting it. . . . For a year now I've been taking out of the library at Cannes all the books written about Christ and Judea, the Chronicles of that time, the Talmud, etc. And so all the details are historically correct, even though I recognize the right of the poet not to follow history in a slavish way.[2]

Thus Kazantzakis maintained that his full-orbed treatment of Jesus faithfully portrays the character of the Jew on whom Christianity is founded, even though he acknowledged his use of poetic license to supplement the meager Gospel accounts. The aim of this chapter is to analyze and appraise the way in which this writer dealt with the sexuality of Jesus, the aspect of Jesus' life that most concerned him.

### "THE LAST TEMPTATION OF CHRIST"

In *The Last Temptation* Kazantzakis used both canonical and apocryphal gospel sources for his account of Jesus' birth. He describes Joseph as old and decrepit when Mary became his wife. On their wedding day a thunderbolt from God struck the couple which simultaneously made Joseph impotent and Mary pregnant.[3] The Virgin Mary had little *rapport* with her miraculously conceived child as he came of age. Embarrassed that he had not found a nice girl to marry, she urged him to select some virgin from her native village of Cana.[4] Jesus rejected this and other expressions of maternal concern. When Mary attempted to rescue her son from an attempted lynching in Nazareth, he scathingly declared: "I have no mother. Who are you?" Later he felt guilty over this alienation and at his crucifixion became reconciled to his embittered mother.[5]

As the title of Kazantzakis' historical novel indicates, Jesus' alleged "last temptation" is the focal point of the book. The Devil's ultimate test was a sexual one. Jesus was placed in seductive situations and tempted to fulfill his strong desire for having coitus and children. He confessed: "When I see a woman go by, I blush and lower my head, but my eyes fill with lust."[6] Satisfying the conjugal urge was, Jesus believed, the primal and persistent human temptation. On seeing snakes slither together into a cluster he reflected: "Men and women couple like this, and that is why God banished us from Paradise."[7]

Jesus' sexual desire was mainly directed toward Mary Magdalene, a daughter of his rabbinic uncle, who lived next door to him in Nazareth.[8] From his earliest memory of her onward, Magdalene had been sensually pleasing. He told of this encounter when he was about three years old: "I took Magdalene by the hand; we undressed and lay down on the ground, pressing together the soles of our naked feet."[9] In the subsequent years of youth these two became self-conscious about their sexuality. Kazantzakis tells of their mutual attraction for one another by alluding to Plato's androgynous tale: "They had both sensed the deep dark fact that one was a man and the other a woman: two bodies which seemed once upon a time to have been one; but some merciless God separated them, and now the pieces had found each other again and were trying to join, to reunite."[10]

Jesus and Magdalene were on the verge of betrothal when the "merciless God" who had willed to separate their bodies confronted him. During that terrifying experience Jesus "shrieked and fell down on his face, frothing at the mouth."[11] Frightened by what he took to be the divine will, he renounced marriage and attempted to exorcise his libido by means of self-flagellation. The celibate kept a nail-studded strap in his carpentry shop and "every evening before he slept he lashed and bled his body so that he would remain tranquil during the night and not act insolently."[12] After dreaming of Magdalene he relieved his shame by scourging himself until his blood spurted out.[13]

This method of rigorous self-punishment left Jesus pale and emaciated but it did not cure his lust. He recalled that Magdalene's father had spoken fondly of a desert monastery to which he belonged until he abandoned the holy life to marry. Jesus wanted to identify himself with monks who "dressed all in white, ate no meat, drank no wine, never touched a woman—did nothing but pray to God."[14] As he headed toward their community he expressed this hope: "There I shall kill the flesh and turn it into spirit."[15]

En route to the monastery he could not resist stopping by to greet Magdalene. Jilted by the one she loved, she had become a prostitute. She explained, "In order to forget one man . . . I've surrendered my body to all men!" Jesus, recognizing that Magdalene's plight was due to his unwillingness to marry her, begged her forgiveness. He found himself craving her body even while visiting her in "the greatest degradation" at a whorehouse where customers were outside awaiting their turn. But because of his determination to remain virginal, he resisted even his desire to touch her lips.[16]

At the monastery beyond Lake Gennesaret he joined with others engaged in self-mortification. Each monk practiced asceticism "so that his soul might be unburdened of the body, might be relieved of this weight and enabled to ascend to heaven in order to find God."[17] John, the son of Zebedee, was also fervently seeking God there. Zebedee believed that his son could have better resolved his frustrations by emulating his father. He admitted: "When I was young there were times when I too got all heated up and twisted and turned on my bed. I thought I was looking for God, but I was really looking for a wife. . . . I got married and calmed down."[18] After a while Jesus felt constrained to leave the secluded life in order to announce throughout the land that God's Messiah had come.

While in progress through Galilee Jesus happened to enter a village where an infuriated crowd had gathered to execute Magdalene. She had been convicted of polluting the Sabbath by failing to rest from selling her body on that day. Jesus exclaimed to those assembled: "Let him among you who is without sin be the first to throw a stone!" He saved her life by making the villagers ashamed of their hypocrisy.[19]

Out of gratitude to Jesus for rescuing her from death, Magdalene gave up prostitution to become a follower of Jesus. Consequently his erotic desire for his repentant cousin became keener than ever. A devilish voice spoke within:

Take her! God created man and woman to match, like the key and the lock. Open her. Your children sit huddled together and numb inside her, waiting for you to blow away their numbness so they may rise and come out to walk in the sun. . . . Look how God married the whore Jerusalem. The nations passed over her, but he married her to save her. Look how the prophet Hosea married the whore Gomer, daughter of Debelaim. In the same way, God commands you to sleep with Mary Magdalene, your wife, to have children, and save her.[20]

Jesus came close to succumbing to this temptation to take Magdalene as his bride, especially since it was subtly couched as an argument from Scripture. On one occasion when Magdalene was hugging his knees "Jesus bent over, took her by the hand and lifted her up. Bashful and enchanted, he held her just as an inexperienced bridegroom holds his bride. His body rejoiced from its very roots."[21]

The most poignant sexual temptation in *The Last Temptation* strikes in the final moments of Jesus' life. While hanging on the cross "the Evil One" enticed him with a "deceptive vision of a calm and happy life."[22] In his imagination Jesus confided to Magdalene: "How very many years I've longed for this moment! Who stepped between us and refused to leave us free—God?" Then he caressed her with joyous abandon. "They lay down under a flowering lemon tree and began to roll on the ground. The sun came and stood above them. A breeze blew; several flowers fell on the two naked bodies. . . . Purring, Mary Magdalene hugged the man, kept his body glued to hers." Afterward in his daydream Jesus confessed: "Beloved wife, I never knew the world was so beautiful or the flesh so holy. . . . I never knew that the joys of the body were not sinful."[23]

But Jesus came out of even this last bout victorious over evil temptation. His conscious mind affirmed after the dream that marriage is basically a lust of the flesh which a holy man must abhor. Kazantzakis' story of Jesus' life concludes: "The moment he cried ELI ELI and fainted, Temptation had captured him for a split second and led him astray. The joys, marriages and children were lies . . . illusions sent by the Devil."[24]

## OTHER TREATMENTS OF JESUS

In works other than *The Last Temptation* Kazantzakis repeatedly attempted to show that genuine imitators of Christ associate purity with sexual abstinence. He saw a reflection of Jesus in Francis of Assisi because he "inwardly transformed all his flesh into spirit" by subduing his id continually.[25] In his novel *Saint Francis,* Kazantzakis pictures a friar who found his affluent family, the prospects of marriage, and all women obstacles to his search for God. Clara, who wanted to marry Francis, was told: "To marry, have children, build a home—I spit on them all!" Again, when she wanted to join his mendicant order, Francis retorted bitterly: "I don't trust you women. Eve's serpent has been licking your ears and lips for too many centuries. . . . Don't touch me!"[26]

Francis' rash responses concealed his inner turbulence. He wondered at times if God's will might not permit a holy man to marry. But more characteristically he attempted to eliminate lust by beating his loins madly and by exposing his naked body in snow until its flesh was blue with cold. Once he had a horrible nightmare after viewing a church fresco representing St. Anthony's temptation. The scene depicted "a blond, naked woman with greedy eyes, pressing her huge breasts against the ascetic's knees," and it stimulated in Francis ambivalent feelings of revulsion and titillation.[27] But Kazantzakis'

Francis, like his Jesus, ended life a hero of faith because he renounced his parents, the woman who loved him, and the opportunity for offspring.

A prominent motif in still another novel, *The Greek Passion*, is that those who represent Jesus in contemporary culture must struggle desperately against their sinful sexuality. This writing of Kazantzakis focuses on the selection of characters for a passion play in a Greek village. Manolios, a humble shepherd, is chosen for the role despite criticism that his engagement to marry renders him unfit. In order to prepare properly for participation, Manolios makes this resolution: "I must . . . keep pure, and not touch a woman. . . . This body isn't mine any longer; it belongs to Christ." His concept of Jesus has been formed by a monastery painting he has seen of a golden-haired young Magdalene darting to embrace the one she loved. But from Jesus' austere mouth issued the words: "Woman, touch me not!"[28]

A tumult rages in Manolios as to whether to play Jesus or to "soil himself" by marrying someone whom he loved and who loved him. He thinks it would be fraudulent to impersonate Jesus after indulging in sexual intercourse, yet the father of his betrothed will not permit a delay in the wedding until after the play is performed. The shepherd's sensual desire causes his face to become swollen with pus. This ugliness makes him so repulsive to his beloved that she rejects him. Manolios interpreted his illness as God's way of saving his virtue, and after his abandonment of marriage his face becomes clear again.[29]

In Kazantzakis' poetic masterpiece, *The Odyssey: A Modern Sequel,* again there are overtones of his fictional treatments of Jesus. The type of Jesus is "a slender virgin-lad" who calls himself "the great ascetic" and affirms, "I've not touched wine or women." He exhorts: "Only he who has never touched the bait of flesh may speak of spirit."[30]

## MISREPRESENTATION OF THE BIBLICAL OUTLOOK

Are these portrayals of Jesus' sexuality anchored in the apostolic testimony to him? Kazantzakis attempted to strip away the perverted interpretations of Jesus which "cassocked representatives of Christianity have heaped upon his figure." Yet he failed in this, for his image of Jesus resembles more a caricature originating in postapostolic tradition than what is disclosed by a scholarly investigation of the New Testament. In treating Francis of Assisi, Kazantzakis was generally faithful to sources contemporary with the saint, but he erred in projecting sexual attitudes of medieval Catholicism back on Jesus.

Kazantzakis not only anachronistically identified Jesus' outlook with that of later Western asceticism but also assumed that it was similar to that of some Eastern holy men. He had studied the sources of Buddhism over many years and had written and rewritten a book on the Buddha.[31] He was in fact so absorbed in the Buddhist *Weltanschauung* that he had Jesus speak of having been previously incarnated. After a period of ascetic renunciation, Kazantzakis' Jesus left his monastic retreat to enable others to become "awake."[32] Kazantzakis shows Buddha as passing up the lures of the evil demon Mara and thereby rejecting the urge to live sensuously with his wife.[33] Both Buddha and Kazantzakis' Jesus attempted to find salvation by extinguishing sensual desires.

Kazantzakis did not realize that Jesus participated in a culture which allied holiness with marital relations rather than with sexual renunciation. The duty of marriage was sanctioned by the first law of the Torah and required of all religious leaders. By no means did the ancient Palestinian Jews believe in lifelong virginity as a life-style for the perfect human being. Kazantzakis held that Adam and Eve were banished from Paradise because they copulated and that their antitypes, Jesus and his mother, restored human salvation because they refrained. That typology, which can be traced to Bishop Iranaeus,[34] seriously distorts Jewish Scriptures and the Gospel sources. It would have been more in accord with the biblical outlook had Kazantzakis held it was the expression of arrogant pride, not love, that caused the loss of Eden. In turn, the ideal society can be restored by the full manifestation of love, marital as well as universal, and by the rejection of hubris. The historical Jesus and Kazantzakis' Jesus were different in that the former did not see women as a symbol of the sensate realm that must be spurned. The moral dualism that was endemic to Greek philosophy and which percolated through Gentile Christianity was not a part of Jesus' ethic. Kazantzakis the Greek betrays his own heritage in assuming that the carnal is tainted, for

Jesus did not impose a dichotomy between the divine spirit and the devilish flesh.

The Palestinian milieu in which Jesus was reared cannot be characterized as either predominantly hedonistic or ascetic. Likewise Jesus did not think that the pursuit of pleasure was the end of life nor did he identify unhappiness with the will of God. Kazantzakis' comprehension of the Gospels is faulty when he interprets Jesus' desire for joy as a manifestation of evil temptation. Jesus' inner struggle is misrepresented by Kazantzakis in this way: "At every opportunity he had to be happy, to taste the simplest human joys—to eat, sleep, to mix with his friends and laugh, to encounter a girl on the street and think, I like her—the ten claws immediately nailed themselves down into him, and his desire vanished."[35] However, the Jesus of the Gospels was noted for his conviviality, for blessing matrimonial unions, and for referring to the wedding feast as a symbol of the highest human happiness.

## AN AUTOBIOGRAPHICAL CONFESSION

Although the Jesus figure in the creative writings of Kazantzakis does not adequately "reincarnate the essence of Christ" as he intended, it reflects clearly a facet of the author's complex personality. Close parallels may be found in his own life for some of the sexual dilemmas his main characters face. In his autobiography, *Report to Greco,* he summed up his life experiences thus: "From my youth onward, my principal anguish, and the well-spring of all my joys and sorrows had been this: the incessant, merciless battle between the spirit and the flesh."[36] His clash began at the age of three with a playmate of the same age who lived across the street. This is how he remembered his early sexual awareness: "We took off our socks, lay down on our backs, and glued our bare soles together. . . . Never in my whole life has a woman given me a more dreadful joy; never have I felt the mystery of the female body's warmth so profoundly."[37] As a schoolboy Kazantzakis was thrilled by legends of the saints' struggles with temptation. Perhaps due to the inhibitions that resulted from taking ascetics as his heroes, he had a traumatic experience after yielding to sexual temptation the first time. Before leaving home for the University of Athens, he and his foreign girl friend hiked to the top of a mountain in Crete and fornicated in a chapel there. Afterward he was aghast as he looked up from the flagstone where he lay: "I discovered Christ eyeing me furiously from the iconostasis. . . . I had suddenly been possessed by an age-old fear: God would hurl a thunderbolt to reduce both of us, the Irish girl and myself—Adam and Eve—to ashes."[38] At the age when Jesus withdrew into the wilderness for forty days Kazantzakis made a pilgrimage to Mt. Athos for the same length of time. He described the principal prohibition enforced at that Greek monastery: "In the thousand years since the Holy Mountain was consecrated to the Virgin, no woman has ever set foot here, no feminine exhalations have soiled the air, not even those of female animals—ewes, nanny goats, hens, or cats."[39] Kazantzakis told of a typical monk there who, after avoiding all feminine contact for decades, was severely shaken emotionally on seeing the exposed breast of a nursing mother.[40] Exalted by "air uncontaminated by woman" at Mt. Athos, Kazantza-kis made this diary entry: "Ah, if I could live always at the peaks! . . . How can I liberate my spirit, how can I break the arrows in my flesh?"[41] Later he visited other monasteries on his home island and as far away as Mt. Sinai. There he commiserated with those who despised the world's joys in order to transubstantiate matter into spirit and wistfully wondered if he could become a monk. But he had too much wanderlust to accept the cloistered life for long.

On leaving the Mediterranean area Kazantzakis traveled exten-sively through Europe. While in Vienna his infatuation with Bud-dhism prompted an attempt to abstain totally from satisfying his sexual appetite.[42] However, having acquired the habit of philander-ing, he soon violated his resolve by arranging to have sexual rela-tions with an acquaintance. Failure to live up to his self-imposed standard caused mental torment and a hideous eczema to bloat his face. A psychiatrist diagnosed this illness as similar to the reported psychogenic cases of some ascetics. In one case a hermit was found to have symptoms of leprosy on his skin while fighting to suppress sensual impulses.[43] As soon as Kazantzakis left the city where the temptress of that occasion lived, "the horrible sexual 'mark' van-ished."[44]

Kazantzakis was torn by two self-images: one a sexually ascetic one, inappropriately represented by Jesus; the other, one of sexual hedonism, appropriately incarnated in Zorba. That lusty friend of Kazantzakis was consumed by an endless succession of ephemeral affairs. He believed that the one unforgivable sin was passing up a coital opportunity. Zorba testified: "If Hell exists, I shall go to Hell . . . not because I've robbed, killed or committed adultery, no! All that's nothing. But I shall go to Hell because one night in Salonica a woman waited for me on her bed and I did not go to her." Reincarnation as a mule was, he suggested, proper punishment for such negligence.[45]

In his odyssey through the cultures of the world Kazantzakis vacillated between the classic poles of Dionysian revelry and Appollonian temperance. At times the wine, women, and song motto of Zorba appealed to him. Kazantzakis admired "the way his body and soul formed one harmonious whole, and all things—women, bread, water, meat, sleep—blended happily with his flesh and became Zorba."[46] But at other times, as we have seen, the opposing tug was always strong.

Kazantzakis ambitiously endeavored to describe the struggles of the historical Jesus. According to the New Testament Jesus "was tempted in every respect as we are" and this writer depicted well a neglected implication of that affirmation. He did not accept the position of Bishop Augustine that Jesus had no libidinous desire. That ascetic argued: since sexual desire pollutes sublime purity, and since Jesus was perfect, ergo he could not have had sexual desire.[47] That syllogism has become accepted dogma in Western Catholicism. Accordingly, *The Last Temptation* was placed on the Index of books with doctrinal errors. Kazantzakis held that Jesus accepted the following viewpoint: since yielding to sexual desire is evil, and since I am seeking to be holy, therefore I cannot engage in coitus, either marital or otherwise. From the standpoint of ancient Jewish culture the major premises of both Kazantzakis' Jesus and Augustine are untrue.

On at least one occasion Kazantzakis rejected the doctrine that sexual intercourse was necessarily contaminated by evil. He stated: "Christianity soiled the union of man and woman by stigmatizing it as a sin. Whereas formerly it was a holy act, a joyous submission to God's will, in the Christian's terror-shaken soul it degenerated into a transgression. Before Christ, sex was a red apple; along came

Christ, and a worm entered that apple and began to eat it."[48] In this assessment Kazantzakis displays that he could not discriminate between the life-style of Jesus and the sexual asceticism that has been prominent in a number of world religious philosophies. All too glibly he assumed that holiness in the Judaism that affected Jesus was defined as withdrawal from the sensuous realm.

Kazantzakis ably articulates the most gnawing heresy in the Christian tradition: the Platonic-Docetic-Gnostic-Manichean syndrome that the sensual is evil and that decontamination is effected by pommeling the pleasure drive to death. That heresy is reflected in the disparaging way "carnal" is defined in dictionaries as "unspiritual" and is made synonymous with "lascivious." In contrast to that persistent position biblical theology affirms that everything is created good and that Jesus is the in*carnal*ity of God. The New Testament witnesses to the way in which the pure Spirit of God has been emptied into the fleshly life of a man. According to the Gospels, Jesus' anguish was over human recalcitrance to extend love more broadly, not over whether to renounce love of a woman.

# EPILOGUE

# *On Imitating Jesus*

THROUGH most of church history few Christians have given full attention to the fact that Jesus was thought of in early Christianity as a man who should be imitated. In the first Christian sermon Peter proclaimed the acts of the man "Jesus of Nazareth."[1] A letter attributed to Peter states: "Christ suffered for you, leaving you an example; you should follow in his steps."[2] Paul affirmed that he imitated the Messiah, and in addressing the Thessalonian Christians he and his associates acknowledged: "You became imitators of us and of the Lord."[3] Bishop Ignatius, in the generation following that apostle, advised those whom he wrote to "imitate Jesus Christ as he imitated his Father."[4] Yet in spite of these and other similar forthright exhortations in the sources of early Christianity, there has been formidable theological and philosophical opposition to accepting the imitation of Jesus as a legitimate approach to Christian conduct.

## RESISTANCE TO IMITATION

Objections to an imitation of Jesus doctrine have been strong from those who think of Jesus more as a discarnate God than as a godly man. Jesus has often been thought of as a supernatural being who has few human characteristics a mortal can copy. An extreme example of this is seen in Docetism, the first major heresy of church history, which held that Jesus had a phantom body. Marcion, the most prominent Docetist, attempted to gather some written sources pertaining to Christ that would advance his interpretation. From Luke's writings he cut out the episodes referring to matters essential to human nature—birth, growth to maturity, and temptations—and began the Gospel with a figure who descended angellike from heaven. He inferred from Luke 8:21 that Jesus had no attachment to women.[5] Marcion was devoted to a vaporous god masquerading as a Palestinian male who was in no way conditioned by human impulses or by ethnic nurture.

New Testament authority Oscar Cullmann has discerned that Docetism "has remained the one great Christological heresy down to this day."[6] Some today as in the past have stressed Jesus' power to the extent of conceiving of him as a mythical Titan who appeared on earth disguised as a peasant. There is a simplistic logic behind this approach: since God is omnipotent, and since Jesus is God, therefore Jesus was not limited by anything human. Many Christians have exalted Jesus' power at the expense of his humanity, even though he is portrayed in the Gospels as a man limited in miraculous powers and as one who gave such healing powers as he possessed a place of secondary importance.[7] If Jesus is viewed as preeminently a miracle worker, he becomes a figure to be awed but not one to be imitated.

Neither is Jesus a pattern to follow for those who attribute to him complete and infallible knowledge. As early as the second century some Christians assumed that Jesus knew from the beginning of his life the whole range of universal wisdom. Accordingly they composed tales of Jesus' childhood in which the wonder boy denounces teachers who have the audacity to suggest that he could learn something he did not know.[8] Church fathers were also reluctant to admit that Jesus lacked full knowledge even though the Gospels state that Jesus "grew in wisdom" as a boy and that as an adult he confessed to his disciples his lack of knowledge pertaining to the future.[9] Augustine admitted that Jesus said he did not know about the timetable for the outcome of history but explained that Jesus was being insincere. According to that bishop, Jesus' ignorance "meant that he was keeping the disciples in ignorance."[10] In order to protect the alleged omniscience of Jesus—a quality never predicated of him by his apostles—Augustine tacitly acknowledged that Jesus was deceptive.

If Jesus had been omniscient, his expressions of surprise and his questions seeking information would have been theatrical.[11] Had Jesus known everything, he could have divulged the cause and the cure for cancer and other diseases. Were it possible to imitate such an unhuman being, could pretending not to know about the future be morally justified? Hardly.

It is not unusual for the founder of a religion to be thought of by devotees principally as a heavenly figure to be worshiped rather than as a human pattern to be imitated. In Buddhism, for example, there has been a pronounced Docetic tendency which minimizes Siddhartha's sharing the human condition. His temporal and spatial qualities have often been replaced by an eternal quality. This has been especially true of the way in which he has been depicted in the *Lotus Sutra,* the most important sacred writing in East Asian Buddhism. Also in the *Mahavastu,* the influential Theravada scripture, Buddha is presented as a person qualitatively different from mortals. It alleges that his conception was not caused by his parents engaging in sexual relations and that he did not possess the natural passions of man.[12]

Although the Docetic interpreter in either Buddhism or Christianity believes he is making the figure he adores more powerful, paradoxically he is attached to a being who is impotent to save. For how can an ethereal Buddha thinly veiled in flesh deliver man from what he has not experienced in any essential way? It is due to this kind of dilemma that a New Testament writer says of Jesus, "Because he himself has suffered and been tempted, he is able to help those who are tempted."[13]

Not only can the alleged omnipotence and omniscience of Jesus be questioned, but also the way his all-goodness is usually interpreted. Some Christians assume that Jesus was unaware of any gap between his ideal self-image and his actual practice, and therefore dismiss as unrealistic the notion of imitating Jesus. To err is human, so how can a being whose conscience is completely clear be a guide to conduct for sinful men?

Although it is perilous to attempt to probe Jesus' self-consciousness, it seems probable that Jesus was unaware of personal sinlessness. He did not assert that he was without sin or that he was God. On the contrary he pointedly differentiated between himself and sublime goodness as well as between himself and God in this terse reply: "Why do you call me good? No one is good but God alone."[14] It is difficult to understand how one who believed he had no imperfections could honestly say those words. Other evidence that Jesus felt a solidarity with sinners is seen in his desire to be baptized. That ceremony was instituted to symbolize the forgiveness of those who were repentant. Moreover, if Jesus had no conscious-

ness of wrongdoing then he could not have sincerely prayed the
"Lord's Prayer." In speaking to his Father in heaven he could have
confessed his virtues but not his sins. Also Jesus could not have
avoided having a self-righteous estimation of himself if he was unaware of unrighteous behavior in his life. Yet Jesus considered self-
righteousness a debilitating vice and taught that the truly good man
is not absorbed in contemplating his own goodness. One of his
parables characterizes the righteous as having no self-consciousness
of their own virtuous deeds.[15] Jesus realized that a person who thinks
he has reached the top of an absolute ethical scale cannot aspire
toward further moral growth.

Even though Jesus seemed unaware of his perfection, it was a
commonplace doctrine in earliest Christianity that he was sinless.[16]
This paradoxical situation is well interpreted by Howard Kee and
Franklin Young: "Perhaps the very fact that Jesus did not claim to
be sinless was crucial to the Christian belief in his sinlessness. For the
crucial point of sinlessness is the possession and enactment of positive virtues such as humility, and an active submission to the will of
God."[17] A somewhat parallel situation is found in comparing a
disciple's evaluation of Socrates with that philosopher's own self-
evaluation. Socrates unassumingly refused to take seriously those
who were of the opinion that he excelled in virtue. He even stated
that he did not know the nature of virtue, much less possess it. Yet
he exemplified such virtues as courage, cheerfulness, and self-discipline in his ordinary conduct of life. Consequently Plato concludes
the account of his teacher's life with these superlatives: "Of all the
men of his time whom I have known, he was the wisest and justest
and best."[18] The irony about morality that surfaces in these illustra-
tions is articulated succinctly by Pascal: "There are only two kinds
of men: the righteous who believe themselves sinners; the rest,
sinners, who believe themselves righteous."[19]

It is unfortunate that some molders of Christian orthodoxy missed
the nuance of the New Testament references to Jesus' moral condition. They also lacked the ethical insight that the best man is the one
most aware of his shortcomings and consequently most receptive to
the grace of God which empowers him henceforth to live a more
perfect life. Augustine followed Origen in holding that Jesus was,
because of a unique disposition of his nature, incapable of sinning.[20]

This position, which has held sway from the fifth to the nineteenth century in Catholic and Protestant Christology, has been incisively criticized by Carl Ullmann: "On the assumption that Jesus was a true, a real man, it cannot of course be denied that it was possible for him to sin."[21] Also, Wolfhart Pannenberg, in the most influential of recent Christological studies, has said: "Jesus' sinlessness is not an incapability for evil that belonged naturally to his humanity but results only from his entire process of life."[22] This position, which puts Jesus in the same category as man, provides a realistic basic for a doctrine of imitation.

Resistance to taking seriously the early Christian's "imitate Jesus" exhortation comes also from the a priori suppositions of philosophers. This may be seen in the outlooks of two of the most eminent Western thinkers. Immanuel Kant had little use for flesh-and-blood exemplars of religious morality. He claims:

There can be no patterns in religion, since the ground, the first principle of behavior must lie in the reason, and it is not to be deduced *a posteriori.* . . . If, then, saintly people are presented to me as models of religion, I must not imitate them, be they ever so holy, I must judge them rather by universal rules of morality. There are, indeed, examples of righteousness, of virtue, and even of holiness, such as the Example set before us in the Gospels, but this Example of the earthly life does not serve as our ground of judgment; rather we judge it by the holy law.[23]

Plato's impact on Kant is clearly evidenced in the priority Kant gives the universal over the particular. That ancient philosopher held that every individual is an imperfect replica of the ideal man who is no-where and no-thing. Those desiring to understand human nature should, Plato thought, transcend the examination of particular copies and intuit the eternal prototype. In a weird metaphor he described man as an inverted plant growing downward from heavenly roots which the divine craftsman formed.[24] According to this metaphysical outlook, the proper way to know true man is to focus on manhood in the abstract and disregard particular men in their environmental setting.

The a priori approach to Christology is most presumptuous because it assumes that the nature of ideal man can be known without empirically studying the life of Jesus in his cultural setting. From the second century to the twentieth some Christian intellectuals have been attracted by Gnostic theology, which contains much of the Platonic theory of reality and accordingly gives scant attention to the historical Jesus. Some scholars approach Christology with a ready-made idealized model of man and then trim the Gospel reports to fit into that Procrustean bed. Jesus thereby often becomes a Docetic person, infinite in knowledge and unperturbed by bodily passions. This approach, starting as it does with a preconceived notion of what goodness is and projecting it onto the founder of Christianity, cannot be reconciled with the New Testament.

## HIS ESSENTIAL CHARACTER

The early Christians viewed the man in Jesus as essential and denounced the Docetic claim that his manhood was incidental. They looked at his person and mission and extrapolated from that unique historical individual the nature of perfect humanity. A splendid example of this approach is seen in the climax of the passion account in the earliest Gospel. While witnessing Jesus' crucifixion a centurion exclaimed, "Truly this man was God's son!"[25] Jesus' divinity and humanity were simultaneously diaphanous: he showed his kinship to God *through* his manhood, not in spite of it. A New Testament letter provides another illustration of the way in which Jesus' greatness is approached through his human accomplishments. "Jesus, during his earthly life, offered up prayers and petitions, with loud cries and tears. . . . Even though he was a son, he learned from what he suffered what it means to obey. By being thus perfected he became the source of enduring salvation to all who obey him."[26] Thus the Jesus of the early Christians was not a quasi-human demigod; rather he was even more of a full-fledged man than his followers.

Claude Welch, one of the most knowledgeable current writers in the field of historical Christology, has made this keen observation regarding Jesus' participation in a certain sociohistorical stream:

He is a Jew of the first century, and to deny this either by implication or silence is to make nonsense of our faith in God's preparation for the coming of the Messiah through the history of Israel. The existence of Jesus as a man in this particular historical situation, with all that that implies by way of limitation and conditioning, is not something merely to be admitted in passing, but to be insisted upon as central to our view of the incarnation. . . . Man exists *qua* man only in and before society. He is defined by the people to which he belongs. He is never man in general, but always man of a particular race, nationality, culture, family, etc. He is inescapably social man, and this means not only that he needs society, but that he is formed and exists in a matrix of social relations.[27]

Welch insists that Jesus, as any man, cannot be understood apart from such social roles as teacher, friend, son, and therapist.

The primacy that Aristotle gave to individual embodiment of the goodness rather than to the abstract form of man is similar to the outlook of the early Christians. In a famous definition he states that moral excellence is "determined by reason *(logos)* as a man of practical wisdom would choose it."[28] For Aristotle whatever is valued by a perfected person is the best criterion for what is right. He observed that imitation of parents, teachers, peers, and historical heroes motivates much of human conduct from childhood onward. That philosopher approved not of a slavish mimicking but of following the regulative principle of the truly virtuous man. A. H. Armstrong points out that for both Aristotle and Christianity "the standard and touchstone of human goodness can only in the last resort be a human character."[29] Christians focus on the divine *logos* that became a human "full of grace and truth."[30] There are some Christian theologians and churches who are emphasizing anew the historical Jesus as an exemplar of morality. They reject the former stress upon Jesus' peculiarities which has made him either so ludicrous or so sublime that most people would not think of imitating him. An eccentric Jesus inspires amusement, disgust, or worship, but little desire for emulation.

Paul's doctrine of Jesus, the second Adam, has been influential on those who are intrigued by a Christocentric ethic. That apostle saw the image of God reflected in all its brilliance in the person of Jesus.[31] By his tragic and triumphant life he brought to full flowering the potentialities of human nature. Consequently he has become the standard for evaluating moral maturity.[32] Kenneth Foreman has commented on Paul's doctrine: "Jesus is the truly *normal*—that is to say, standard—human being. To become like him, to belong to his family rather than to that of Adam the First, is not to become freakish and abnormal; it is to discover what being human really is."³³ Likewise, the United Presbyterians in their new confession of faith begin their description of Jesus in this way: "In Jesus of Nazareth true humanity was realized once for all. Jesus, a Palestinian Jew, lived among his own people and shared their needs, temptations, joys, and sorrows."³⁴

According to that Pauline perspective, Jesus is on center, not ec-centric, *vis à vis* authentic human nature, and it is the purpose of the Gospel to enable people "to be conformed to the image of God's son."³⁵ In a word, the more Christlike, the more human. Conversely, people are qualitatively abnormal to the extent that they do not inculcate Jesus' life-style, even though their mores may well be average on some quantitative scale.

The prime values intrinsic to the life of Jesus are sketched in 1 Corinthians 13. Jesus was posing in the studio of Paul's mind when he painted his artistic masterpiece. For that apostle he personified the *agape* of God, so Paul's ode to love may be read with this legitimate substitution of subject:

Jesus is patient and kind. He is not jealous; neither is he ostentatious, nor snobbish, nor rude. Jesus is not selfish; neither is he touchy, nor resentful; he does not gloat when others go wrong—on the contrary, he is gladdened by goodness. Jesus is cautious in exposing; he is eager to believe the best, always hopeful, conquering through endurance.

Jesus may be compared to Mount Everest inasmuch as his virtues are the summit of the human spirit. Many who remain at a great distance are inspired by what they have heard about him from those who have traveled along the "Way." Some are attracted to the foothills to view his towering grandeur from a first-hand study. A few climb the ardous trail to the peak which seems to touch heaven. There they briefly look out at the world from that exhilarating lofty perspective, for none have the endurance to stay permanently in that rarefied atmosphere.

Whether one should or should not try to imitate Jesus is not the question for those who are committed to New Testament Christianity. Rather the issue is this: to what degree of specificity should this imitation be carried? James Gustafson's discussion of Jesus' personal possessions helps to clarify this question. He writes:

A life ideal, given in some detail, is bound to mirror both the more trivial characteristics of the time from which it is drawn, and the more significant determinative patterns that emerge from its particular definitions of issues. For example, does the following of Jesus as moral ideal require that one dress as men did in Judea and Galilee at that time? Obviously, no. But does the picture of Jesus require that the follower dress simply, without expensive adornment, without luxury? Is simplicity in manner and style of life the proper inference for those who would follow one who had no place to lay his head, and who told his disciples to take but one tunic with them in their ministry? If it is, the Christian moral ideal in our time would run strongly against the cultural and economic stream which presses more and more consumer goods into life, without regard for simplicity, not to mention self-denial.[36]

In order to imitate Jesus we also need to perform the delicate surgery of separating the incidental and dated form from the essential and timeless content. No one thinks that the imitation of Jesus means the wearing of a tasseled shawl and few think that it means the literal washing of one another's feet. It is true that Jesus said after washing his disciples' feet in the Upper Room: "I have given you an example, that you also should do as I have done to you."[37] But it is apparent to most interpreters that we have here a graphic demonstration to reinforce Jesus' advocacy of mutual service. Due to modern technology which makes roads less dusty, footwear more comfortable, and journeys by foot uncommon, it is a rare dinner guest who needs or wants a soothing and cleansing footwashing. Therefore to indulge in a practice common to ancient Palestine, as a few sects occasionally still do, is an archaic ritual which may accomplish little more than give participants the ego-satisfaction of following Jesus literally. Reenacting that once-needed custom may fall short of stimulating the imagination to discover culturally equivalent actions which would be more truly imitative of Jesus in current society. Cleaning up a ghetto playground or assisting a family-forsaken elderly person are contemporary ways in which the footwashing obligation might be discharged.

The imitation possibilities of other sayings and actions of Jesus are more problematic. Regarding some aspects of his conduct it is difficult to ascertain the way in which he related himself to his own culture, not to mention how he might have related himself to contemporary society. One facet that is currently much debated is Jesus' association with political movements. Was he a passive non-resister of the Roman army of occupation in Palestine or a sympathizer of the Zealot guerrillas who were devoted to Jewish liberation? There are some episodes in the Gospels in which instruments of violence seem to be sanctioned for use, but other teachings in which they are not.[38] The prevailing opinion of Christian ethicists, and probably the correct one, is that Jesus condoned a nonvengeful self-defense for one's community so long as it was based on a long-range concern for reconciliation.

Those who attempt to imitate Jesus have also had difficulty in comprehending Jesus' attitude toward self-mortification. Some have found the essential character of Jesus best expressed in the wilderness temptation episode. It is recorded that Jesus "fasted forty days and forty nights."[39] From the medieval era onward many pious Christians have attempted to copy that fasting model during the forty days of Lent. A few have pressed this strenuous asceticism further by making the continued abhorrence of pleasures a dominant feature of the Christian life-style. The most noted illustration of this outlook is found in the fifteenth-century writing, *On the Imitation of Christ*. Regarding that book Charles Eliot has asserted: "With the exception of the Bible, no Christian writing has had so wide a vogue or so sustained a popularity."[40] Its alleged author, the monk Thomas à Kempis, described Jesus as one who dedicated his life to abstaining from physical pleasures.[41] Accordingly, the devout man should despise "this miserable flesh."[42] Also he should withdraw from public life, for it is better to have fellowship with God than with men.[43]

Protestants have generally rejected the picture à Kempis draws of Jesus, even though they assume that the genuine Christian life is one that follows the life of Jesus. John Calvin, for example, says that "God the Father . . . has in Christ stamped for us the likeness to which he would have us conform. . . . Christ, through whom we return into favor with God, has been set before us as an example, whose pattern we ought to express in our life."[44] Yet Calvin rejects fasting as a "holy imitation of Christ" because "it is plain that Christ did not fast to set an example for others."[45] Rather, a man who aspires to imitate Jesus should cherish and help others as though they were members of his own body.[46]

Protestant ethicist Gustafson has tellingly assessed the Jesus portrayed by à Kempis: "The Christ who is imitated is hardly one we recognize in the Gospels or the rest of the New Testament." In the image of perfection projected by à Kempis, Gustafson continues, there is a false "cleavage between the realm of the spirit—peace, true joy, the soul, all that is good; and the realm of the flesh—passions, senses, 'the world,' and all that is evil."[47] The sense-shunning Jesus of à Kempis is even more extreme than John the Baptist. Yet according to the Gospels, Jesus was faulted by some of his contemporaries for being more convivial than John and for disregarding the practice of fasting.[48] To imitate Jesus means to affirm the joyful life, not renounce it.

## HIS SEXUALITY AND OURS

This discussion of the imitation of Jesus will be completed with a consideration of the relevance of Jesus' sexuality for his followers. What bearing do his attitudes and his practices in that area have on Christian morality? The signifiance of his attitudes toward the opposite sex is easily discernible. Catholic theologian Leonard Swidler expresses one implication: "Jesus vigorously promoted the dignity and equality of women in the midst of a very male-dominated society: Jesus was a feminist, and a very radical one. Can his followers attempt to be anything less—*De Imitatione Christi?*"[49] Also the positive attitude that Jesus had toward weddings, marriage, and children shows that there is no basis for Christians to depreciate those who marry.

But what guidance, if any, can be found in Jesus' actual marital status for the life-style of his followers? The lack of explicit information in the historical sources regarding the way he expressed or did not express his sexuality complicates the issue. Different individuals and sects have thought of him as a self-made eunuch, a celibate, a monogamist, a polygamist, or an unmarried philanderer. Only the first three possibilities have been given any serious attention. The third type which maintains that Jesus practiced monogamy can be subdivided into those who conjecture that he was a widower who may have remarried, or that he lived as a bachelor after his wife deserted him, or that he lived with one wife throughout his adult life. The different ways in which Jesus could have expressed or contained his sexuality will now be examined from the standpoint of their plausibility and their significance for those who regard him as the pattern of the moral life.

What particular behavioral modifications have resulted in those who have assumed Jesus to have castrated himself? Origen, one of the most influential theologians in the patristic era, mutilated himself in a frenzied effort to suppress his lust and imitate one who he thought was literally a eunuch.[50] The cult of Cybele was prominent in Egypt where Origen lived, and he probably interpreted the story of Jesus with the mythology of Attis in mind. Cybele priests castrated themselves on the assumption that it aided in attaining perfection and because they believed that the shepherd Attis emasculated himself. Like those pagan priests, Origen believed that the elimination of sexual functioning was the foremost of living sacrifices pleasing to God.[51]

In the eighteenth and nineteenth centuries there was in Russia a sect of Skoptzy (that is, "castraters") who baptized converts by mutilating male and female genitals with a red-hot iron and by amputating breasts.[52] They believed that they were imitating Jesus, who actually became a eunuch according to their allegation.[53] The horrendous conduct of those people illustrates the double error of first misinterpreting a teaching of the gospel and then engaging in a cruel practice antithetical to the compassionate spirit of Jesus. Exegetes are virtually unanimous that Jesus was not encouraging castration when he spoke favorably about eunuchs or when he said, "It is better for you to lose one part of your body than for the whole of it to be thrown into hell."[54]

Nearly all Christians have interpreted the words attributed to Jesus regarding "those who have made themselves eunuchs" as referring to himself and to other men who abstain from genital sexuality for reasons other than physical mutilation. Pope Paul VI presents the usual interpretation of the Matthean eunuch passage in his encyclical on priestly celibacy. He cites it as his principal authority for claiming that "Christ remained throughout his whole life in a state of celibacy" and for lauding those who imitate his renunciation of "the bonds of flesh and blood."[55] From the third century to the present day most Christians have thought that Jesus lived the "eunuch" life because he had no desire for fleshly relations with a woman and/or because being a husband and father are unworthy roles for one who is totally devoted to doing God's will.

Those who assume that Jesus abstained from marriage have often appealed to his life-style to justify sexual asceticism. Basil, Jerome, Augustine, and Methodius, who strongly influenced the spread of the monastic movement, looked to a celibate Jesus as the exemplar of their holier way of life. Augustine, for example, exhorted: "We are to contemplate in Christ himself the chief instruction and pattern of virginal purity."[56] Methodius even went so far as to claim that virgins, "not bearing the pains of the body for a little moment of time but enduring them through all their life," imitate Jesus better than the martyrs of the church.[57] Those prelates glibly believed that the single person necessarily suffered more than a married man and that Jesus, who carried the most painful burden possible, must have been unmarried.

How true to human experience is the notion that the unmarried person suffers more than the married? A sample of opinions expressed across the centuries show that there is at least as much basis for affirming the opposite contention. Chrysostom wrote:

It is a grievous thing to have children, still more grievous not to have any; for in the latter case marriage has been to no purpose, in the former a bitter bondage has to be undergone. If a child is sick, it is the occasion of no small fear; if he dies an untimely death, there is inconsolable grief; and at every stage of growth there are various anxieties on their account, and many fears and toils.[58]

In Spanish folk literature there is a tale about a harried husband who, after hearing a preacher recount all the torments that Jesus endured before his death, inquired if Jesus was married. On being told that he never had a wife, the married man concluded that Jesus could not have known the depth of suffering.[59] In a similar vein the contemporary novelist Kingsley Amis has stated that a celibate Jesus would have avoided what is for most people the most testing of all human experiences—close ties with spouse and children. Amis claims that the zenith and nadir of one's humanity are best disclosed in a person beset by the obligations of the marriage bond. On the other hand, the bachelor is deluded who asserts that he has renounced family responsibilities for the more demanding call of God.[60] These several opinions fall short of demonstrating that the married life as such is more burdensome than the single life and thereby is more in accord with what is expected of the disciple who has been asked to "carry his cross." They do illustrate, however, the absurdity of the frequent claim by celibates that their way is in general more arduous than that of men who live with the inevitable domestic conflict situations and discharge their duties as husband, father, and son-in-law.

Even if Jesus were as a matter of fact unmarried, what significance should that have for the life-style of Christians? Is marriage—with its agonies and ecstasies—such a profound experience that Christians should reject Jesus as a viable pattern to be copied? This seems to be the outlook of the married Catholic theologian Daniel Callahan when he writes: "It is almost impossible for a contemporary man to model his life on Christ's. Most of us will marry."[61]

Another approach to an alleged unmarried Jesus would be to stress that Christians should pattern their lives after only those qualities of his which are essential to full humanity. It could well be claimed that being a complete human does not depend upon experiencing either marriage or old age. Through misfortune rather than intent one or both of these experiences might be missed. Jesus did not experience the difficulties of old age, but that fact need not make him less relevant as a pattern for the aged to imitate. Likewise, marriage is a nonessential for complete humanity, so a married or unmarried person of either sex has an equal potential for re-presenting Jesus, the paradigm of true manhood.

In Judaism marriage has wrongly been viewed as prerequisite to self-realization. Due to the need for many offspring in the underpopulated ancient world it is understandable that marriage was regarded as obligatory for all humans. The perspective of classical Judaism is expressed in the judgment that "the Divine Presence rests only upon a married man, because an unmarried man is but half a man."[62] Less stringently Rabbi Robert Gordis, in a recent essay urging the "re-Judaizing" of Christianity, states: "Judaism regards marriage and not celibacy as the ideal human state, because it alone offers the opportunity for giving expression to all aspects of human nature."[63]

Islam has followed its parent Semitic religion in making marriage obligatory. In the *Koran,* Mohammed is recorded as having said: "Those of you who are unmarried shall marry."[64] Those who imitate the life-style of that frequently espoused prophet are expected to marry at least once.

Traditional Islam and Judaism have gone to an extreme in requiring marriage and in assuming that the humanity of an unmarried adult is necessarily diminished. It is both uncharitable and unwise, for example, to maintain that Beethoven, a lifelong bachelor, who was warmly disposed toward matrimony, is less an expression of ideal manhood than Bach, who married twice and had twenty children. Erasmus and Pope John XXIII are likewise superb examples of the human spirit, even though, as Catholic priests, they did not marry.

William Hoyt has defended the resolve to remain single as an expression of one's sexuality in this way:

Does one have to be sexually active to be sexually authentic? Rather, is it not the fully sexed person who can decide what his sexual role will be without feeling the need to prove to himself or anyone else that he is virile? . . . One may ask whether the unofficial but widely enforced rule that Protestant minister must marry has always had wholesome results. A man can be called to be a minister without being called to be a husband and father.[65]

Protestant Hoyt is properly concerned about the fact that the sanctions prompting his fellow clergyman to marry are, in many instances, almost as rigid as the mandatory requirement of celibacy in the Catholic priesthood. As Charles Smith says of his fellow Protestant ministers, "A clergyman who remains unmarried for more than a year after graduation from seminary is suspected of being abnormal, immoral or chicken."[66]

Now that the reproductive function of marriage is no longer primary, it can be seen more clearly that the life of bachelors or those earlier stigmatized as "spinsters" need not be less than fully human. Indeed, in light of the ominous overpopulation problem on our globe, a Christian might decide that he can best express the "mind of Christ" by choice of the single status. Judging by the sharp increase in the number of single adults reported by recent United States census figures, there are a growing number who are opting to remain unmarried. However, modern medical technology has effectively isolated the procreative from the other functions of marriage. Methods of birth control have given individuals the freedom to decide the question of marriage independently from the question of adding new life to a crowded world. In this regard it is instructive to realize that Jesus emphasized companionship rather than procreation as the basic purpose of marriage.

So long as it is recognized that Jesus was a sexual being and had a warm appreciation of marriage, his actual marital status is incidental to his full humanity and to his role as model of Christian morality. With regard to that status it is interesting to note that the earliest and most recent interpretations of the "eunuch" saying of Matthew show that it did not refer to lifelong celibacy. Contemporary Catholic exegetes Jacques Dupont and Quentin Quesnell agree with church fathers Justin Martyr and Clement of Alexandria in holding that the saying has reference to a man who lives in continence after being deserted by his wife.[67] Due to his resolve to seek for mutual forgiveness and reconciliation with his spouse, he rejects remarriage.

The only interpretation of this passage that makes sense in the context of the teaching on marriage in Matthew 19 is that Jesus is commending those men married to unfaithful wives who patiently and chastely await the return of their prodigal spouses.[68] There is no explicit indication in the passage that Jesus was referring to his own marital status or to that of any other particular persons. However, since many who attempt to imitate Jesus have assumed that he identified himself with the "eunuchs," how should this affect their lifestyle? Surely there is no encouragement here for a married person to separate from his spouse and renounce marriage. Rather it places high value on the permanence of the marriage covenant and says in effect that the married Christian should accept severe deprivation and humiliation if that is necessary for restoring a broken marriage.

Some contemporary theologians who have reflected seriously on Jesus' marital status have rightly held that it is a historical detail that should have no bearing on the life-style of his followers. Charles Davis, after acknowledging that the "historical probabilities favor marriage rather than celibacy," goes on to comment: "If he was married, his marriage was a particular fact about him in his cultural context: no evidence makes it an essential feature of his personal religion."[69] The imitation of Jesus' doctrine should be relevant to the situation of all Christians regardless of whether they are single, married, separated, or divorced. Also, assuming that the divine incarnation could have been as fully expressed in a feminine form, it is not basic to Christianity that its founder was masculine. G. W. H. Lampe defines in this excellent way what it should mean to follow Jesus: "It means the imitation of his total commitment to God, his obedience to God's will, and his attitude of unswerving love for others which was the fruit of his openness to God. . . . The Christian is called, not to reproduce the externals of the life of Jesus, but to live in the spirit of Jesus."[70]

Undiscriminating attempts to duplicate Jesus' pattern of life without attention to the different contextual situations of his culture and one's own can do violence to the personal liberty valued by Jesus and the apostles. If historical probability favors a married Jesus, as I think a judicious examination of the life and times of Jesus suggests, this subverts the Christian celibate's claim that he is following Jesus' pattern more closely. But it should not cause the married Christian to engage in the similar error of narrowly assuming that the married life is necessarily holier because Jesus was married. The pattern given by Jesus is not of a cookie-cutter type but one exemplifying how the most godlike life has been fleshed out by an individual in a concrete environment. One of the challenges of the Christian life is to discern what elements of Jesus' life are dated and dispensable forms and what are integral and essential qualities of the life of God's people.

The New Testament testifies that Jesus came "to set at liberty those who are oppressed" and says that "where the spirit of the Lord is, there is freedom."[71] Consequently, those who accept Jesus as the model of the Christian life should maximize responsible freedom. Unless the imitation of Jesus is interpreted broadly, it can involve the surrender of individuality and make a travesty of Christian freedom.

There should be no more reason for a chaste person to have feelings of anxiety over abstaining from marriage than for a vegetarian to feel guilty about renouncing meat. Likewise, those who indulge in marriage and those who enjoy meat should recognize that while their life-styles are the most common types, they are not necessarily the only healthy kinds of behavior. Unwholesome-

ness results from those who become celibates or who fast on the one
hand, and from those who become married or reject dietary restrictions on the other hand, because they believe their personal choice
to be morally and religiously superior to the alternative ways of life.
There are overtones in Paul's counsel of tolerance for assessing the
single or non-single status:

Let the vegetarian not hold in contempt the meat eater, and let him who
does eat meat not pass judgment on him who does not; for God has accepted
him. . . . The meat eater has the Lord in mind, since he gives thanks to God;
while he who abstains has the Lord in mind no less, since he too gives thanks
to God. . . . I know and am persuaded by the Lord Jesus that nothing is
intrinsically defiled.[72]

It may be provident that there is no explicit comment in the New
Testament regarding the way in which Jesus physically expressed his
sexuality. For if the records of earliest Christianity had called attention to his marital status then church leaders might have erected an
immutable doctrine that the sexual life-style required for the holier
life is whatever Jesus was declared to have had. As it is, each Christian is free to evaluate the proddings of his own flesh-spirit and
resolve what his or her life-style will be.

# NOTES

### Introduction: Jesus, Religion, and Sexuality

1. *Time*, June 21, 1971, cover article, pp. 56–63.
2. J. A. T. Robinson, *The Human Face of God* (Philadelphia, 1973), p. 63..
3. J. Blenkinsopp, *Sexuality and the Christian Tradition* (Dayton, Ohio, 1969), p. 81.
4. Cf. 1 Cor. 1:23.
5. Mark 3:5.
6. Matt. 23:13, 23, 25, 27, 29; 21:12.
7. Matt. 5:22.
8. Matt. 5:28.
9. J. Burckhardt, *On History and Historians* (New York, 1965), pp. 37–38.
10. G. B. Shaw, Preface of "Getting Married" in *Bernard Shaw* (New York, 1962), 4:323.
11. Shaw, Preface of "Androcles and the Lion," ibid., 5:388.
12. R. Linton, "Universal Ethical Principles" in R. Ashen, ed., *Moral Principles of Action* (New York, 1952), p. 651.
13. *The Gaina Sutras* in *Sacred Books of the East* (Oxford, 1884), 22:21, 48, 207.
14. H. C. Warren, ed., *Buddhism in Translations* (Cambridge, 1947), p. 61.
15. M. K. Gandhi, "Self-Restraint vs. Self-Indulgence," in R. Duncan, ed., *Selected Writings of Mahatma Gandhi* (London, 1951), pp. 159–64; cf. Erik H. Erikson, *Gandhi's Truth* (New York, 1969), pp. 142, 236–37.
16. Cf. E. F. Dakin, *Mrs. Eddy* (New York, 1929), pp. 307–20.
17. M. B. Eddy, *Science and Health* (Boston, 1875), pp. 68, 475.
18. W. H. Masters and V. E. Johnson, *Human Sexual Inadequacy* (Boston, 1970), p. 229.
19. S. Hiltner, "For Faith and Fulfillment," *Presbyterian Outlook*, January 4, 1971, p. 5.
20. Vatican II, "Decree on Priestly Formation," sec. 10; Paul VI, *Sacerdotalis Caelibatus* 5, 12, 22; cf. *Time*, September 21, 1970, p. 62.
21. Cf. *New York Times*, August 9, 1971.
22. A. H. Silver, *Where Judaism Differed* (New York, 1956), p. 198.

23. D. Flusser, *Jesus* (New York, 1969), p. 7.

24. *Jewish Quarterly Review* (1894), p. 381.

25. Lactantius, *Divine Institutes* 6, 23.

26. Origen, *Genesis Homilies* 5, 4.

27. W. N. Pittenger, *Christology Reconsidered* (London, 1970), p. 61.

28. E. g., see reviews by Charles Davis, in the London *Observer,* March 28, 1971, (reprinted in *The Critic,* March-April 1972, pp. 57–60) and Frederick C. Grant, *Churchman* (March 1971). Since publishing *Was Jesus Married?* I have learned that Schalom Ben-Chorin in *Bruder Jesus: Der Nazarener in Jüdishcher Sicht* (Munich, 1967) earlier and independently came to a similar conclusion. That Jerusalem scholar has written: "I am convinced that Jesus of Nazareth, like any rabbi in Israel, was married. His apostles and opponents would have mentioned it, if he had differed from the general custom" (p. 129).

29. Hilary, *The Trinity* 35.

30. Augustine, *Incomplete Work Against Julian* 4, 57.

31. L. E. Keck, *A Future for the Historical Jesus* (New York, 1971), p. 34.

32. R. Gordis, "Re-Judaizing Christianity," *Center Magazine* (September 1968), pp. 10, 13.

33. W. N. Pittenger, *The Christian Understanding of Human Nature* (Philadelphia, 1964), p. 72.

### *Chapter 1. Jesus' Dual Paternity*

1. C. Y. Glock and R. Stark, *Religion and Society in Tension* (Chicago, 1965), p. 95.

2. T. Boslooper, *The Virgin Birth* (Philadelphia, 1962).

3. H. von Campenhausen, *The Virgin Birth in the Theology of the Ancient Church* (Naperville, Ill., 1964).

4. Gen. 29:31; 30:22.

5. Ps. 139:14.

6. Ex. 14:21; 15:8.

7. E. g., 1 Sam. 5:6; 2 Chron. 26:20; Ex. 4:11.

8. E. g., Gen. 6:3; Job 27:3.

9. Isa. 32:15; 44:3–4; Ps. 104:30.

10. Job 33:4.

11. Hosea 1:10; cf. Deut. 14:1; Isa. 43:6.

12. *Kiddushin* 30b.

13. I. Abrahams, "Marriage (Jewish)," *Encyclopedia of Religion and Ethics* (Edinburgh, 1905).

14. *Genesis Rabbah* 8, 9.

15. G. F. Moore, *Judaism* (Cambridge, 1927), 1:437; J. Abelson, *The Immanence of God in Rabbinical Literature* (London, 1912), p. 207.

16. *Aboth* 3:2; cp. Matt. 18:20.

17. *Sotah* 17a.

18. Philo, *On the Decalog* 107; *On the Special Laws* 2, 2, 225.

19. Philo, *On Abraham* 254.

20. Philo, *On the Change of Names* 131, 137.

21. Philo, *On the Cherubim* 40–47. Philo lived in Alexandria, and may also have been influenced by the traditional Egyptian outlook on procreation. In the fourteenth century B.C. this hymn to the god Aton was attributed to Pharoah Ikhnaton: "Creator of seed of women,/Thou who makest fluid into man,/Who maintainest the son in the womb of his mother. . . ." (J. B. Pritchard, ed., *Ancient Near Eastern Texts* [Princeton, 1955], p. 370.) Although this poem does not indicate it, human and divine paternity were not considered mutually exclusive. "In Egyptian thought, the natural act of procreation was also an act of god" (Boslooper, op. cit., p. 166).

22. Rom. 1:3–4.

23. Gal. 4:5–6; Rom. 8:15, 19.

24. John 1:13, 18, 45.

25. John 3:6–7.

26. Matt. 1:1–17; 13:55.

27. W. E. Phipps, *Was Jesus Married?* (New York, 1970), pp. 42–43. Also, Irenaeus states that the Ebionites, a Jewish Christian sect, accepted only the Gospel of Matthew and that they did not believe that Jesus was virginally conceived (*Against Heresies* 3, 11, 7; 5, 1, 3). This indicates that for at least a century after the composition of Matthew its nativity stories had not been interpolated to carry a doctrine of Mary's virginal conception.

28. C. T. Davis, "Tradition and Redaction in Matthew 1:18–2:23," *Journal of Biblical Literature* (December 1971), pp. 412–13.

29. Luke 4:22.

30. E. g., B. H. Streeter, *The Four Gospels* (London, 1936), p. 268; F. C. Grant, *An Introduction to New Testament Thought* (Nashville, 1950), p. 230; R. Bultmann, *The History of the Synoptic Tradition* (Oxford, 1968), pp. 291, 304.

31. Cf. A. Plummer, *St. Luke* (New York, 1922), pp. 30–31.

32. E. g., P. Winter, "The Proto-Source of Luke 1," *Novum Testamentum* (1956), pp. 184–85; J. Moffatt, *An Introduction to the Literature of the New Testament* (New York, 1918), p. 267.

33. Judg. 13:2–25.

34. Deut. 22:23–24; 2 Sam. 3:14; Philo, *On the Special Laws* 3, 12; E. Neufeld, *Ancient Hebrew Marriage Laws* (London, 1944), p. 144.

35. *Kethuboth* 1, 5; *Yebamoth* 4, 10. Cohabitation within a year of betrothal was required (*Kethuboth* 5,2). For Tobias it happened on the same day (Tobit 7–8).

36. Ex. 21:10; cp. 1 Cor. 7:3.

37. M. Cohn, "Marriage," *The Universal Jewish Encyclopedia* (New York, 1948).

38. *"Parthenos"* in *Theologisches Wörterbuch zum Neuen Testament,* ed. G. Kittel (Stuttgart, 1933- ).

39. Gen. 34:3; Homer, *Iliad* 2, 514; Sophocles, *Trachiniae* 1219; Aristophanes, *Nubes* 530; J. H. Moulton, *The Vocabulary of the Greek Testament* (London, 1930); H. J. Leon, *The Jews of Ancient Rome* (Philadelphia, 1960), pp. 130, 232; cf. J. M. Ford, "The Meaning of 'Virgin,' " *New Testament Studies* 12 (July, 1966): 293–99.

40. Ruth 3:9; Ezek. 16:8.

41. G. B. Caird, *The Gospel of St. Luke* (New York, 1963), p. 31.

42. Cf. W. Eichrodt, *Theology of the Old Testament* (Philadelphia, 1961), pp. 152, 223.

43. Cf. Boslooper, op. cit., pp. 31–41.

44. Ignatius, *Trallians* 9, 1.

45. Ignatius, *Ephesians* 18, 2.

46. Ignatius, *Smyrnaeans* 1, 1.

47. Aristides, *Apology for the Christians to the Roman Emperor* 15, 1.

48. Justin, *Dialogue with Trypho* 48, 54.

49. Justin, *Apology* 1, 33.

50. Justin, *Dialogue with Trypho* 67.

51. Justin, *Apology* 1, 21.

52. Cf. E. R. Goodenough, *The Theology of Justin Martyr* (Jena, 1923), pp. 181, 238.

53. Tertullian, *Apology* 21, 9–14.

54. Plutarch, *Life of Alexander* 2.

55. Cf. A. J. Toynbee, *A Study of History* (London, 1939) 1: 267–69.

56. Jerome, *Against Jovinian* 1, 42.

57. Porphyry, *Life of Pythagoras* 2.

58. Diogenes Laertius, *Lives of the Philosophers* 3, 2.

59. Suetonius, *Lives of the Caesars* 2, 94.

60. Philostratus, *Apollonius of Tyana* 1, 4, 6.

61. Pseudo-Justin, *On the Resurrection* 3.

62. T. Walker, *Is Not This the Son of Joseph?* (London, n.d.), pp. 33–34.

63. *Gospel of Philip*, Saying 6.

64. Ibid., 82, 91.

65. Ibid., 17.

66. Athanasius, *The Incarnation of the Word of God* 8, 5.

67. K. Barth, *Church Dogmatics* (Edinburgh, 1956) 1/2: 192–94.

68. Augustine, *Against Julian* 5, 14.

69. J. A. T. Robinson, "Our Image of Christ Must Change," *Christian Century* 90 (March 21, 1973): 340.

70. Cp. C. Darwin, *The Descent of Man* in R. M. Hutchins, ed., *Great Books of the Western World* (Chicago, 1952), 19:593.

## Chapter 2. The Maturing of Rabbi Jesus

1. E. E. Malone, "Aureole," *New Catholic Encyclopedia* (New York, 1966).

2. D. Laertius, *Lives of the Philosophers* 8, 19.

3. Deut. 22:12; cf. E. Schürer, *A History of the Jewish People in the Time of Jesus Christ* (New York, 1891) 2:2, 111–12.

4. Matt. 9:20; 14:36.

5. A. Edersheim, *The Life and Times of Jesus the Messiah* (New York, 1900) 2:15.

6. Ibid., 1:xiii.

7. Lev. 19:18; *Sifra on Deuteronomy* 41.

8. G. F. Moore, *Judaism in the First Century of the Christian Era* (Cambridge, 1927) 2:127.

9. *Kiddushin* 76b.

10. Cf. Gen. 17:25; 34:14–19; Ex 4:26; J. P. Hyatt, "Circumcision," *Interpreter's Dictionary of the Bible* (New York, 1962).

11. Philo, *On the Special Laws* 1, 4–7.

12. Gen. 17:9–14.

13. *Genesis Rabbah* 46, 4.

14. M. Buber, *Israel and the World* (New York, 1948), p. 181

15. D. Mace, *The Christian Response to the Sexual Revolution* (New York, 1970), p. 20.

16. Ex. 13:11–15; Lev. 12:2–8; Luke 2:21–24.

17. H. Danby, *The Mishnah* (London, 1933), p. 793.

18. *Hagigah* 1, 1.

19. Josephus, *Against Apion* 1, 12.

20. Deut. 6:7.

21. Philo, *Embassy to Gaium* 31.

22. Cf. Moore, op. cit., 2:202.

23. *Taanit* 23a.

24. *Berakoth* 3, 3; Eighteen Benedictions 5–6.

25. E. g., Sirach 4:10.

26. *Aboth* 5, 21.

27. Jer. *Kethuboth* 32c; cf. Moore, op. cit., 3:104.

28. Cf. Sirach 5:23.

29. Cf. Moore, op. cit., 1:314.

30. *Niddah* 5, 6.

31. Josephus, *Life* 2.

32. Josephus, *Against Apion* 2, 19.

33. R. M. Grant, *The Earliest Lives of Jesus* (New York, 1961), pp. 14, 38–49.

34. Luke 2:46.

35. Cf. Deut. 6:20–21; R. de Vaux, *Ancient Israel* (New York, 1965), p. 49.

36. Sirach 6:34–35.

37 *Aboth* 2, 5; cp. Matt. 5:1–5.

38. Tobit 4:15; *Shabboth* 31a; cp. the positive expression of this "Golden Rule" in Matt. 7:12.

39. John 7:15.

40. Moore, op. cit., 1:320; cf. Acts 22:3.

41. J. Klausner, *Jesus of Nazareth* (New York, 1925), p. 409.

42. D. Flusser, *Jesus* (New York, 1969), p. 18.

43. *Tosefta Kiddushin* 1, 11.

44. *Aboth* 2, 2.

45. *Yoma* 35b.

46. Gal. 1:14; Acts 18:3.

47. Mark 6:3; Matt. 13:55.

48. *Aboth* 4, 5.

49. *Yebamoth* 62b.

50. Cf. W. E. Phipps, *Was Jesus Married?* (New York, 1970), pp. 22–33, 47.

51. *Yebamoth* 6, 6.

52. C. G. Montefiore, *The Synoptic Gospels* (London, 1927) 2:265.

53. E. g., Prov. 5:18–19; Song of Songs.

54. *Kiddushin* 4, 13.

55. S. Ben-Chorin, *Bruder Jesus: Der Nazarener in Jüdischer Sicht* (Munich, 1967), p. 128.

56. *L' Osservate Romana,* March 10, 1971; cp. P. M. Rinaldi, Letter to the Editor, *New York Times,* January 29, 1971.

57. Luke 3:23; 4:32, 36.

58. G. Bornkamm, *Jesus of Nazareth* (New York, 1960), p. 96; W. D. Davies, *Christian Origins and Judaism* (Philadelphia, 1962), p. 20.

59. R. Bultmann, *Jesus and the Word* (New York, 1958), p. 58.

60. Luke 9:33, cp. Mark 9:5; Luke 18:41, cp. Mark 10:51.

61. Cf. Moore, op. cit., 3:15.

62. Matt. 23:5–12.

63. Assumption of Moses 7:9–10.

64. Psalms of Solomon 4:7, 22.

65. Cf. Moore, op. cit., 2:190–93.

66. Jer. *Berachoth* 14b.

67. *Berachoth* 34b.

68. *Yoma* 39b; *Hagiga* 17b; *Taanith* 25b; *Baba Metzia* 59b.

69. *Leviticus Rabbah* 10, 111d.

70. Matt. 12:27; cf. Mark 9:38; Josephus, *Antiquities* 8, 2, 5.

71. Mark 12:34.

72. Matt. 23:3.

73. Matt. 5:20; Luke 11:42.

74. Cf. *Shabbath* 1, 5–8.

75. Mark 2:27; *Mekilta on Exodus* 31, 13.

76. Klausner, op. cit., p. 278; cf. Moore, op. cit., 2:31; Flusser, *Jesus,* p. 48.

77. *Yoma* 8, 6; *Shabbath* 7, 2.

78. *Hagigah* 1, 8.

79. Mark 2:23–28; 1 Sam. 21:1–6.

80. Matt. 12:1–8.

81. Mark 1:22.

82. Cf. F. J. Foakes Jackson and K. Lake, *The Beginnings of Christianity* (London, 1920) 1:291.

83. Moore, op. cit., 1:61.

84. John 7:49.

85. *Aboth* 2, 6.

86. *Aboth* 3, 11; *Demai* 2, 2–3.

87. *Tohoroth* 4, 5.

88. *Pesahim* 49a; Deut. 27:21.

89. Cf. Mark 7:15.

90. Mark 2:17.

91. Ezek. 34:16.

92. C. G. Montefiore, *Some Elements of the Religious Teaching of Jesus* (London, 1910), p. 57.

93. Matt. 13:52.

94. Phil. 3:5; Gal. 1:14.

95. *Berachoth* 47b.

96. Mark 2:22.

97. Luke 4:18; Isa. 61:1.


## Chapter 3. *Jesus the Philogynist*

1. J. Jeremias, *Jerusalem in the Time of Jesus* (Philadelphia, 1969), p. 376; so also R. Bultmann, *Jesus and the Word* (New York, 1958), p. 61.

2. Luke 8:3; 22:27.

3. Luke 10:1–9.

4. 1 Cor. 9:5; 16:19; Rom. 16:3; Acts 18:2, 18–19.

5. Acts 18:26.

6. Clement of Alexandria, *Miscellanies* 3, 6, 53.

7. Luke 23:27–28.

8. Abelard, *Letters* 7; Rom. 8:35.

9. Philo, *On the Creation* 165.

10. Josephus, *Against Apion* 2, 25.

11. *Tosephta Berakhoth* 7, 18.

12. *Kiddushin* 82b.

13. "Gunē" in *Theologisches Wörterbuch zum Neuen Testament,* ed. G. Kittel (Stuttgart, 1933– ).

14. Sirach 25:24–26; 42:13–14.

15. Charles Wesley, *Short Hymns on Select Passages of Holy Scripture.*

16. R. Grimm, *Love and Sexuality* (New York, 1964), p. 40.

17. Deut. 22:22; Ezek. 16:38–40.

18. *Sotah* 1, 5–6.

19. *Sotah* 3, 4; Num. 5:16, 24, 27.

20. John 8:7.

21. C. K. Barrett, *The Gospel According to St. John* (London, 1956), p. 491.

22. G. F. Moore, *Judaism in the First Century of the Christian Era* (Cambridge, 1927), 2:270.

23. Philo, *On the Special Laws* 51.

24. Sirach 9:3.

25. R. C. Leslie, *Jesus and Logotherapy* (New York, 1965), pp. 53–54.

26. *Gettin* 9, 10.

27. *Yebamoth* 14, 1.

28. Mark 10:10–12.

29. Cf. W. E. Phipps, *Was Jesus Married?* (New York, 1970), pp. 84–86.

30. Matt. 19:4–5.

31. Mark 12:40.

32. Luke 18:2–5.

33. J. Jeremias, *The Parables of Jesus* (New York, 1963), p. 153.

34. H. E. Fosdick, *The Man from Nazareth* (New York, 1949), p. 148.

35. D. Sayers, *Are Women Human?* (Grand Rapids, Mich., 1971), p. 47.

36. Luke 2:42–51.

37. Luke 11:27–28.

38. Mark 3:21, 31–34.

39. John 2:4; 19:26–27.

40. Mark 14:9; John 12:1–3.

41. Mark 14:6.

42. Mark 11:11; 14:3; Luke 10:38; John 11:18.

43. Luke 7:46.

44. Ps. 23:5.

45. E. g., Song of Songs 1:3; Ruth 3:3; Esther 2:12.

46. *Shabbath* 23, 5.

47. Mark 14:7–8.

48. *Sotah* 3, 8.

49. E. g., Tertullian, *On Purity* 11; Clement of Alexandria, *The Instructor* 2, 8, 61; J. N. Sanders, "Those Whom Jesus Loved," *New Testament Studies* 1 (1955), pp. 38–41; C. H. Dodd, *Historical Tradition in the Fourth Gospel* (Cambridge 1963), pp. 162–73; J. L. McKenzie on Matt. 26:6 in *The Jerome Biblical Commentary* (Englewood Cliffs, N.J., 1968).

50. Jeremias, *Jerusalem*, p. 375.

51. Luke 10:39.

52. Acts 22:3.

53. Cf. Betty Friedan, *The Feminine Mystique* (New York, 1963).

54. Quoted in A. F. Tyler, *Freedom's Ferment* (Minneapolis, 1944), p. 431.

55. *Aboth* 1, 5.

56. *Jerusalem Sotah* 19a; cf. *Sotah* 3, 4.

57. Luke 10:42.

58. Matt. 15:39.

59. Luke 8:2.

60. Mark 15:40–41.

61. Matt. 26:56.

62. C. H. Dodd, *The Interpretation of the Fourth Gospel* (Cambridge, 1958), p. 441.

63. Origen, *Against Celsus* 2, 55.

64. E. Renan, *The Apostles* (New York, n. d.). p. 49.

65. Ibid., p. 70.

66. John 20:18; 1 Cor. 9:1.

67. Acts 26:12–19.

68. E. g., Luke 1:11; 9:31; 22:43; 24:34; cf. *horao* in *Theologisches Wörterbuch zum Neuen Testament*, ed. G. Kittel (Stuttgart, 1933– ).

69. Job 42:5. (Italics mine.)

70. Isa. 6:1. (Italics mine.)

71. John 20:17.

72. E. g., Mark 5:28; 1 Cor. 7:1. Also in classical Greek (Plato, *Laws* 840a) and in the Septuagint (Gen. 20:6; Prov. 6:29) the verb could refer to sexual intercourse.

73. J. Marsh, *The Gospel of St. John* (Baltimore, 1968), p. 637; cf. C. K. Barrett, *The Gospel According to St. John* (London, 1956). p. 470.

74. 2 Cor. 5:16; 1 Cor. 15:44.

75. Luke 20:34–36.

76. Cf. Tobit 12:19.

77. Matt. 28:20.

78. Luke 24:11, 22.

79. Josephus, *Antiquities* 4, 8, 15; cp. *Shebuoth* 4, 1.

80. E. g., J. H. Bernard, "International Critical Commentary," *Gospel According to St. John* (Edinburgh, 1928), p. 413; David Smith, *In the Days of His Flesh* (New York, n. d.), pp. 202–211.

81. Cf. R. M. Grant, *After the New Testament* (Philadelphia, 1967), p. 193.

82. Cf. Gregory the Great, *Sermons* 25, 1, 10; "Mary Magdalen," *The Catholic Encyclopedia* (New York, 1910).

83. J. M. Murry, *Jesus, Man of Genius* (New York, 1926), p. 328; Asch, *The Nazarene* (New York, 1939); D. Sayers, *The Man Born to Be King* (London, 1943), p. 183; F. Mauriac, "Life of Jesus," *The Critic* (September-October 1972), pp. 24–25.

84. K. Gibran, *Jesus* (New York, 1928), pp. 13–15.

85. J. B. Mayor, "Mary Magdalene," *Hastings Dictionary of the Bible* (Edinburgh, 1900).

86. *Gospel of Philip*, Saying 32; cf. W. E. Phipps, *Was Jesus Married?* (New York, 1970), pp. 136–37.

87. Mark 15:40–41; Matt. 27:56; Luke 8:2, 24:10

88. Julian, *Convivium* 336.

89. F. Nietzsche, *Antichrist* secs. 48, 56.

90. H. L. Mencken, *In Defense of Women* (New York, 1963), p. 142.

91. J. Langdon-Davies, *A Short History of Women* (New York, 1927), p. 202.

92. Quoted in G. MacEoin, "Unequal in the Sight of God," *McCall's* magazine (June 1971), p. 79.

93. O. A. Piper, *The Biblical View of Sex and Marriage* (New York, 1960); p. 97; cp. K. Barth, *Church Dogmatics* (Edinburgh, 1961) 3/4: 150–81.

94. C. S. Lewis, *Christian Behavior* (London, 1943), p. 36.

95. B. Graham, "Jesus and the Liberated Woman," *Ladies' Home Journal* (December 1970), p. 42.

96. S. D. Collins, "Women and the Church: Poor Psychology, Worse Theology," *Christian Century* (December 30, 1970), p. 1558.

97. Cf. Eleanor Flexner, *Century of Struggle* (Cambridge, 1959), pp. 74, 80, 89.

98. Cf. Edith Deen, *Great Women of the Christian Faith* (New York, 1959), pp. 394–96.

99. E. Kedourie, *Nationalism in Asia and Africa* (New York, 1970), p. 118.

100. *Koran* 4:34; Stanley Lane-Poole, *The Speeches and Table Talk of the Prophet Mohammed* (London, 1882), p. 161.

101. Cf. Thomas Berry, *Religions of India* (New York, 1971), p. 66.

102. K. S. Latourette, *The History of the Expansion of Christianity* (New York, 1944), 6:200.

103. *Maha-Parinibbana-Sutta* 5, 23.

104. *The Analects* 17, 25.

105. May-ling S. Chiang, *This Is Our China* (New York, 1940), p. 174.

106. *Women and the Way* (New York, 1938), p. 32.

107. D. Mace, *The Christian Response to the Sexual Revolution* (Nashville, 1970), p. 78.

108. H. Phillips in *The Interpreter's Bible* (Nashville, 1951), 6:612.

109. L. Swidler, "Jesus Was a Feminist," *Catholic World* (January 1971), p. 179.

110. K. L. Woodward, "From Adam's Rib to Women's Lib," *McCall's* magazine (June 1971), p. 118.

## Chapter 4. Ascetic Philosophers on Sexuality

1. 1 Cor. 9:5.

2. J. Gibbons, *The Faith of our Fathers* (Baltimore, 1895), p. 456.

3. J. W. Rehage, "Celibacy, Canon Law of," *New Catholic Encyclopedia* (New York, 1966).

4. Xenophon, *Memorabilia* 2, 1, 6.

5. W. James, *The Varieties of Religious Experience* (New York, 1902), pp. 272–76.

6. H. D. F. Kitto, *The Greeks* (Harmondsworth, Eng., 1951), p. 176.

7. E. Hamilton, *The Greek Way to Western Civilization* (New York, 1952), p. 164.

8. F. Nietzsche, *The Birth of Tragedy;* E. R. Dodds, *The Greeks and the Irrational* (Berkeley, 1951).

9. Plato, *Cratylus* 400c.

10. Aristotle, *Metaphysics* 986a.

11. Diogenes Laërtius, *Lives of Eminent Philosophers* 8, 9, 42.

12. Hippolytus, *Refutation of All Heresies* 7, 17; *Lives* 8, 54.

13. Dodds, op. cit., p. 155.

14. Strobaeus, *Anthology* 3, 18; 4, 24.

15. Epicurus, "Letter to Menoeceus," *Lives* 10, 132.

16. Diogenes Laërtius, op. cit., 10, 4.

17. *Ibid.,* 10, 118–19.

18. Lucretius, *The Nature of the Universe* 4, 1115–18.

19. Plato, *Phaedrus* 233.

20. G. M. A. Grube, *Plato's Thought* (Boston, 1958), p. 114.

21. Plato, *Phaedrus* 250, 253.

22. Plato, *Phaedo* 64, 82.

23. Plato, *Laws* 839.

24. B. A. G. Fuller, *History of Greek Philosophy* (New York, 1931), pp. 445–46.

25. Plato, *Republic* 451–56.

26. Plato, *Timaeus* 90.

27. Plato, *Republic* 402–405.

28. Ibid., 559.

29. Ibid., 485.

30. C. Brinton, *A History of Western Morals* (New York, 1959), p. 93.

31. Plato, *Republic* 329.

32. Aristotle, *Nicomachean Ethics* 1152b.

33. Aristotle, *On The Generation of Animals* 737a.

34. Aristotle, *Politics* 1254b, 1260a; Sophocles, *Ajax* 293.

35. Aristotle, *Nicomachean Ethics* 1162a.

36. I. Singer, *The Nature of Love* (New York, 1966), p. 96.

37. Diogenes Laërtius, op. cit., 6, 29.

38. Ibid., 6, 54.

39. Ibid., 2, 36–37.

40. Athenaeus, *Banquet of the Learned* 13, 588.

41. Augustine, *City of God* 14, 20.

42. C. H. Moore, "Greek and Roman Ascetic Tendencies," in H. W. Smyth, ed., *Harvard Essays on Classical Subjects* (Cambridge, 1912), p. 120.

43. Epictetus, *Discourses* 3, 12, 24.

44. Epictetus, *Manual* 40.

45. Epictetus, *Discourses* 1, 18; *Manual* 33.

46. Diogenes Laërtius, op. cit., 7, 113, 117.

47. Cf. S. Sandmel, *Philo's Place in Judaism* (Cincinnati, 1956), p. 211; E. R. Goodenough, *An Introduction to Philo Judaeus* (New Haven, 1940), p. 160; F. W. Farrar, *History of Interpretation* (New York, 1886), pp. 137–38, 142.

48. Eusebius, *Ecclesiastical History* 2, 4.

49. Philo, *On the Migration of Abraham* 9.

50. Philo, *Allegorical Interpretation* 3, 22.

51. Philo, *Questions on Exodus* 1, 7.

52. Philo, *On the Creation* 165.

53. Cf. H. A. Wolfson, *Philo* (Cambridge, 1962) 2:231.

54. Philo, *Allegorical Interpretation* 3, 45.

55. W. Windelband, *History of Ancient Philosophy* (New York, 1899), p. 343.

56. Philostratus, *Apollonius of Tyana* 1, 13.

57. K. S. Guthrie, *Numenius of Apamea* (London, 1917), p. 97, 133.

58. Plutarch, *On the Control of Anger* 464b.

59. Cf. Frederick Copleston, *A History of Philosophy* (New York, 1962) 1/2:197.

60. Henry Chadwick, *The Sentences of Sextus* (Cambridge, 1959), p. 138, Sentence 273.

61. Smyth, op. cit. p. 136.

62. Plotinus, *Enneads* 3, 5, 1.

63. Ibid., 3, 5, 2.

64. Porphyry, *Life of Plotinus* 2, 37.

65. A. H. Armstrong, *An Introduction to Ancient Philosophy* (Boston, 1959), p. 196.

66. Porphyry, *On Abstinence* 4, 20.

67. Ibid., 4, 7.

68. Cf. H. Cherniss, *The Platonism of Gregory of Nyssa* (Berkeley, 1930), p. 62.

69. Plato, *Phaedrus* 246.

70. Gregory of Nyssa, *On Virginity* 12.

71. Ibid., 21.

72. Augustine, *Against Julian* 4, 14, 72; cf. Cicero, *On Offices* 1, 30.

73. Augustine, *City of God* 14, 16.

74. F. Nietzsche, *Beyond Good and Evil*, Preface.

75. Augustine, *City of God* 14, 17–18.

76. Augustine, *On Marriage and Concupiscence* 2, 5.

77. Augustine, *Against Julian* 4, 16.

78. Ibid., 5, 8.

79. Cf. N. P. Williams, *The Ideas of the Fall and of Original Sin* (London, 1927), p. 366.

80. Augustine, *On Marriage and Concupiscence* 1, 13.

81. Augustine, *City of God* 14, 26.

82. Augustine, *The Good of Marriage* 10.

83. A. Harnack, *History of Dogma* (London, 1898) 2, 1, 1, *n.*

84. Augustine, *On Christian Doctrine* 3, 8.

85. Plato, *Symposium* 190.

86. Gregory of Nyssa, *On Creation of Man* 16.

87. Gregory of Nyssa, *The Great Catechism* 16.

88. Erigena, *De Divisione Naturae* in J. P. Migne, ed., *Patrologia Latina* 122, 571c.

89. Ibid., 122, 836a.

90. Ibid., 122, 541a, 815c.

91. Aquinas, *Summa Theologica* 2–2, q. 152, 1.

92. Ibid., q. 151, 3; Augustine, *Soliloquies* 1, 10.

93. Aquinas, op. cit., 3, q. 49, 6; Jerome, *Against Jovinian* 1, 49; Sextus, *Sentence* 231.

94. Aquinas, op. cit., 1, q. 98, 2; cf. Augustine, *De Genesi ad litteram* 9, 5, 9.

95. Ibid., 1, q. 99, 2; Aristotle, *History of Animals* 574a.

96. Aquinas, op. cit., 2–2, q. 26, 10; Aristotle, *On the Generation of Animals* 729a.

97. Aquinas, op. cit., 3, q. 32, 4.

98. I. Kant, *Lectures on Ethics* (New York, 1963), p. 164.

99. I. Kant, *The Science of Right*, sec. 24.

100. Kant, *Lectures on Ethics*, p. 170.

101. A. Schopenhauer, *The World as Will and Idea* (London, 1883), 1:506.

102. Ibid., 1:491.

103. Ibid., 1:524.

104. Ibid., 3:448.

105. Ibid., 1:524.

106. Ibid., 3:352, 448.

107. Ibid., 1:114–20.

108. Cf. H. R. Hays, *The Dangerous Sex* (New York, 1964), pp. 207–209.

109. R. G. Smith, ed., *Søren Kierkegaard: The Last Years* (New York, 1965), pp. 77–79, 171.

110. Ibid., p. 120.

111. Ibid., p. 265.

112. W. Lowrie, *Kierkegaard* (New York, 1938), p. 19.

113. Ibid., p. 132.

114. P. P. Rohde, *Søren Kierkegaard* (New York, 1963), p. 66.

115. A. Dru, ed., *The Journals of Søren Kierkegaard* (New York, 1938), pp. 538–39.

116. Smith, op. cit., p. 115.

117. Rohde, op. cit., pp. 69–70.

118. J. Hohlenberg, *Søren Kierkegaard* (New York, 1954), p. 119.

119. Cf. V. Eller, *Kierkegaard and Radical Discipleship* (Princeton, 1968), p. 241.

120. Smith, op. cit., pp. 266–67.

121. M. Buber, *Between Man and Man* (London, 1947), pp. 51–52.

122. S. Kierkegaard, *Attack Upon Christendom* (New York, 1944), pp. 213–22; cf. George Arbaugh, *Kierkegaard's Authorship* (Rock Island, Ill., 1967), p. 369.

123. Smith, op. cit., p. 119.

124. Kierkegaard, op. cit., p. 213.

125. Plato, *Phaedo* 66–67.

126. F. Nietzsche, *The Genealogy of Morals* 3, 7.

127. D. H. Lawrence, *A Propos of Lady Chatterley's Lover* (New York, 1953), p. 118.

128. Aquinas, op. cit., 1, q. 54, 5.

129. A. Schopenhauer, "Essay on Women" in D. H. Parker, ed., *Schopenhauer Selections* (New York, 1928), pp. 436–44.

130. J. S. Mill, "The Subjection of Women;" F. Nietzsche, *Beyond Good and Evil*, ch. 7.

131. Cf. O. Zöckler, "Asceticism (Christian)," *Encyclopedia of Religion and Ethics* (New York, 1928)—a summary of his *Askese und Mönchtum* (Frankfort, 1897); J. Leipoldt, *Griechische Philosophie und Früchristliche Askese* (Berlin, 1961), pp. 31, 60.

132. W. E. Phipps, *Was Jesus Married?* (New York, 1970), pp. 15–119.

133. E. Brunner, *The Divine Imperative* (Philadelphia, 1947), p. 364.

134. Clement of Alexandria, *Miscellanies* 3, 3, 21.

135. Tertullian, *On Prescription Against Heretics* 30.

136. Ambrose, *Duties of the Clergy* 1, 258.

## Chapter 5. The Reformers on Sexuality

1. M. Luther, "Exhortation to All Clergy" in T. G. Tappert, ed., *Selected Writings of Martin Luther* (Philadelphia, 1967), p. 92.

2. H. T. Lehman, ed., *Luther's Works* (Philadelphia, 1957), 54: "Table Talk," n. 3777.

3. M. Luther, *Commentary on Galatians*, 5:17.

4. J. Atkinson, ed., *Luther's Works* (Philadelphia, 1966), 44, p. 178.

5. Lehman, ed., op. cit., 54: "Table Talk," n. 1472, recorded by John Schlaginhaufen.

6. Cf. O. Lahteenmaki, *Sexus und Ehe bei Luther* (Turku, 1955), pp. 45, 66, 139.

7. T. G. Tappert, ed., *Letters of Spiritual Counsel* (Philadelphia, 1955), p. 273.

8. Written in the Luther room at Wartburg, according to the *Oxford Dictionary of Quotations* (London, 1941). E. Simon notes in *Luther Alive* (New York, 1968), p. 337: "If Luther was not the author of this jingle, long attributed to him, both form and sentiment bear his stamp."

9. 1 Cor. 7:2–5; Ex. 21:10.

10. R. Lewinsohn, *A History of Sexual Custom* (New York, 1958), p. 177.

11. Cf. J. Pelikan, ed., *Luther's Works* (St. Louis, 1955), 12:348.

12. *D. Martin Luthers Werke* (Weimar, 1884), 2:168.

13. Quoted in J. Atkinson, *Martin Luther and the Birth of Protestantism* (Baltimore, 1968), pp. 247–48.

14. W. H. Lazareth, *Luther on the Christian Home* (Philadelphia, 1960), p. 209.

15. *Augsburg Confession*, Art. 23.

16. *Formulary of Concord*, 1577.

17. Erasmus, "On Letter Writing" in R. H. Bainton, *Erasmus of Christendom* (New York, 1969), pp. 49–50.

18. P. Schaff, *History of the Christian Church* (Grand Rapids, Mich., 1958), 8:6.

19. *Zwinglis Sämtliche Werke*, 7:110, as quoted in H. J. Hillerbrand, *The Reformation* (New York, 1964), pp. 115–16.

20. Schaff, op. cit., p. 53. Thesis n. 49.

21. T. M. Lindsay, *A History of the Reformation* (New York, 1925), 2:36–37.

22. H. Zwingli, *Of the Education of Youth*, part 2.

23. Conclusions of Berne, n. 9, as quoted in J. H. Leith, *Creeds of the Church* (Garden City, 1963), p. 130.

24. H. Zwingli, *An Account of the Faith*, point 4.

25. Cf. W. G. Cole, *Sex in Christianity and Psychoanalysis* (New York, 1955), p. 131; D. S. Bailey, *Sexual Relation in Christian Thought* (New York, 1959), p. 173.

26. J. Calvin, *Institutes*, 2, 1, 4, 9.

27. Ibid., 4, 19, 34.

28. J. Calvin, *Commentary on 1 Timothy*, 5:9–13.

29. Jerome, *Letters* 123, 13.

30. W. Tyndale, *Treatises* (Cambridge, 1848), 1:438.

31. Jerome, *Against Jovinian* 1, 3; *Letters* 22, 20.

32. J. Calvin, *The First Epistle of Paul the Apostle to the Corinthians* (Grand Rapids, 1960), pp. 11–12.

33. Cf. Calvin, *Institutes* 4, 19, 34; M. Luther, *Pagan Servitude of the Church*, 6.

34. Quoted in W. Walker, *John Calvin* (New York, 1906), p. 236.

35. R. M. Frye, "The Teachings of Classical Puritanism on Conjugal Love," *Studies in the Renaissance* 2 (1955):155.

36. R. V. Schnucker, *Views of Selected Puritans, 1560–1630, On Marriage and Human Sexuality* (University of Iowa dissertation, 1969). Microfilm.

37. E. Sirluck, ed., *Complete Prose Works of John Milton* (New Haven, 1959) 2:235, 246.

38. J. Calvin, *Commentaries on Genesis* (Grand Rapids, Mich., 1948), 1:134.

39. J. Milton, *Paradise Lost* 4:728, 738–43, 770–75.

40. Ibid., 503, 750.

41. Ibid., 744–47.

42. C. Hodge, *Systematic Theology* (New York, 1895) 3:368–71.

43. P. Tillich, *A History of Christian Thought* (New York, 1968), pp. 110, 127.

44. 1 Peter 3:7.

## Chapter 6. *William Blake on Joseph's Dilemma*

1. T. J. J. Altizer, *New Apocalypse: The Radical Christian Vision of William Blake* (East Lansing, 1967); J. G. Davies, *The Theology of William Blake* (Oxford, 1948); J.M. Murry, *William Blake* (New York, 1964).

2. Luke 7:37–50.

3. W. Blake, *There Is No Natural Religion,* "Application." All citations are from G. Keynes, ed., *The Complete Writings of William Blake* (London, 1966).

4. Irenaeus, *Against Heresies* 3, 19, 1.

5. Athanasius, *The Incarnation of the Word of God* 9.

6. Matt. 1:18–19.

7. W. Blake, *The Everlasting Gospel,* sec. i.

8. Cf. M. D. Johnson, *The Purpose of the Biblical Genealogies* (Cambridge, 1969), p. 178.

9. Gen. 38:24–26; Josh. 2:1; 2 Sam. 11.

10. W. Blake, *Jerusalem,* plate 62; *The Four Zoas,* line 365.

11. Cf. C. K. Barrett, *The Gospel According to St. John* (London, 1956), p. 288. However, in the same context Jesus is also given this insult: "You are a Samaritan." These malicious charges are more likely directed toward the community in which Jesus was reared than toward his conception. Jesus, a non-Judean, is accused of mixed ancestry.

12. Cf. J. Klausner, *Jesus of Nazareth* (New York, 1925), pp. 35–46.

13. Origen, *Against Celsus* 1, 32.

14. Tertullian, *The Shows* 30.

15. W. Blake, *Letter to James Blake,* January 30, 1803.

16. *The Everlasting Gospel,* sec. e, i.

17. N. Frye, *Fearful Symmetry* (Boston, 1962), p. 120.

18. Deut. 22:23–24; John 8:4–5.

19. *Jerusalem,* 61.

20. *The Everlasting Gospel,* Prologue.

21. W. Blake, *Songs of Experience,* "Ah! Sun-Flower."

22. *Jerusalem,* 60.

23. Ibid., a.

24. Ibid., 7.

25. Titus 1:15.

26. Murry, op. cit., p. 287.

27. Luke 6:36.

28. Mark 14:36. *Abba* is the familial form of "father" in Aramaic, Jesus' mother tongue.

29. Matt. 9:13; 21:31.

30. *The Everlasting Gospel,* sec. e.

31. Heb. 4:15.

32. *The Everlasting Gospel,* sec. e, i.

33. *Jerusalem,* 61.

34. Hosea 1:9–2:17.

35. Ibid., 3:1.

36. Ezek. 16.

37. Isa. 54:8.

38. Heb. 11:31; Luke 1:48.

39. Klausner, op. cit., pp. 232–33.

### *Chapter 7. D. H. Lawrence's Appraisal of Jesus*

1. Cf. V. Mehta, "The New Theologian," *The New Yorker,* November 20, 1965, pp. 78–80.

2. J. A. T. Robinson, *Honest to God* (Philadelphia, 1963), p. 120.

3. H. Davies, "The God of Light and the Dark Deities," *Religion in Life* 38 (1969): 230, 241.

4. *The Later D. H. Lawrence* (New York, 1959), pp. 412, 411.

5. Ibid., p. 442.

6. Ibid., p. 414.

7. D. H. Lawrence, *Lady Chatterley's Lover* (New York, 1957), p. 266.

8. Rom. 6:5.

9. F. D. McDonald, ed., *Phoenix: The Posthumous Papers of D. H. Lawrence* (New York, 1936), pp. 737, 739.

10. *The Later D. H. Lawrence,* p. 425.

11. Ibid., p. 433.

12. Ibid.

13. Ibid., pp. 442, 443.

14. Ibid., pp. 444–45.

15. Ibid., p. 391.

16. A. L. Webber and T. Rice, "Jesus Christ Superstar," Decca Records, 1970.

17. D. Krook, *Three Traditions of Moral Thought* (Cambridge, 1959), p. 286.

18. Luke 5:34; 7:31–34.

19. Davies, op. cit., p. 235.

20. R. D. Sturm, "Lawrence: Critic of Christianity," *Catholic World* 208 (November 1968): 76.

21. *Yadayim* 3, 5. There is no firm evidence that the Song was interpreted allegorically in Akiba's era, so his remark probably referred to the passionate human love expressed in it.

22. John 3:16; Mark 12:30–31; 1 Cor. 13.

23. Luke 7:47; John 11:5.

24. Col. 3:19.

25. D. Peerman, "D. H. Lawrence: Devout Heretic," *Christian Century* 78 (1961): 237.

26. H. T. Moore, ed., *Collected Letters of D. H. Lawrence* (New York, 1962), 1:180.

27. W. R. Hoyt, "Re 'D. H. Lawrence's Appraisal of Jesus,' " *Christian Century* 88 (1971): 861–62.

28. S. Freud, *An Outline of Psychoanalysis* (New York, 1949), p. 109.

29. W. R. D. Fairbairn, *Psychoanalytic Studies of the Personality (London, 1952), pp. 35, 40;* cf. the special Fairbairn issue of the *British Journal of Medical Psychology* 36 (June 1963).

30. E. Fromm, *The Art of Loving* (New York 1963), p. 19.

31. D. H. Lawrence, "A Propos of Lady Chatterley's Lover," in H. T. Moore, ed., *Sex, Literature, and Censorship* (New York, 1953), p. 96.

32. *The Later D. H. Lawrence*, p. 386.

## Chapter 8. Kazantzakis on Jesus' Sexuality

1. N. Kazantzakis, *The Last Temptation of Christ* (New York, 1960), pp. 2, 3 (hereafter cited as LTC).

2. Quoted in Helen Kazantzakis, *Nikos Kazantzakis* (New York, 1968), p. 505 (hereafter cited as NK).

3. LTC, pp. 30, 134.

4. LTC, p. 26.

5. LTC, pp. 311, 44a.

6. LTC, p. 146.

7. LTC, p. 150.

8. LTC, p. 42.

9. LTC, p. 145.

10. LTC, p. 42; cf. Plato, *Symposium*, 190.

11. LTC, p. 26.

12. LTC, p. 13.

13. LTC, p. 81.

14. LTC, pp. 66–67.

15. LTC, p. 82.

16. LTC, pp. 90, 87, 94.

17. LTC, p. 99.

18. LTC, p. 131.

19. LTC, . 176.

20. LTC, p. 257.

21. LTC, p. 329.

22. LTC, p. 3.

23. LTC, pp. 448–50.

24. LTC, p. 496.

25. N. Kazantzakis, *Report to Greco* (New York, 1965), p. 379 (hereafter cited as RG).

26. N. Kazantzakis, *Saint Francis* (New York, 1962), pp. 114, 228.

27. Ibid., pp. 220, 286.

28. N. Kazantzakis, *The Greek Passion* (New York, 1953), p. 92.

29. Ibid., pp. 94–106, 226.

30. N. Kazantzakis, *The Odyssey: A Modern Sequel* (New York, 1958), 21:1130–1325.

31. NK, p. 80.

32. LTC, pp. 269, 333.

33. N. Kazantzakis, *Zorba the Greek* (New York, 1952), pp. 19, 113–14 (hereafter cited as ZG).

34. Irenaeus, *Against Heresies* 5, 19, 1.

35. LTC, p. 27.
36. RG, p. 290.
37. RG, p. 47.
38. RG, p. 130.
39. RG, pp. 197–98.
40. RG, p. 228.
41. Quoted in NK, p. 55.
42. NK, p. 81.
43. RG, pp. 354–55.
44. NK, p. 83.
45. ZG, pp. 103, 106–107.
46. ZG, p. 132.
47. Augustine, *Against Julian* 5, 8, 15.
48. RG, p, 371.

### Epilogue: On Imitating Jesus

1. Acts 2:22.
2. 1 Peter 2:21.
3. 1 Cor. 11:1; 1 Thess. 1:6.
4. Ignatius, *To the Philadelphians* 7:2.
5. Tertullian, *Against Marcion* 4, 7, 19.
6. O. Cullmann, *Christ and Time* (Philadelphia, 1950), p. 128.
7. E. g., Mark 6:5; Luke 4:40–44; 11:29.
8. Cf. *Gospel of Thomas* 6.
9. Luke 2:40; Mark 13:32.
10. Augustine, *On the Trinity* 1, 23.
11. E. g. , Mark 6:6; 9:21.
12. Cf. T. Berry, *Religions of India* (New York, 1971), pp. 166–69.
13. Heb. 2:18.
14. Mark 10:17–18.
15. Matt. 25:37–39.
16. 2 Cor. 5:21; 1 John 3:5; 1 Peter 2:21–24; Heb. 4:15.
17. H. C. Kee and F. W. Young, *Understanding the New Testament* (Englewood Cliffs, N. J., 1957), p. 86.
18. Plato, *Phaedo* 118.
19. Pascal, *Pensées* 533.
20. Origen, *On First Principles* 2, 6, 5; Augustine, *On the Sinful State* 2, 11, 16.
21. C. Ullmann, *The Sinlessness of Jesus* (Edinburgh, 1870), p. 163.
22. W. Pannenberg, *Jesus—God and Man* (Philadelphia, 1968), p. 363.
23. I. Kant, *Lectures on Ethics* (New York, 1963), pp. 109–110.
24. Plato, *Timaeus* 90.
25. Mark 15:39.
26. Heb. 5:7–9.
27. C. Welch, *The Reality of the Church* (New York, 1958), pp. 90–91.
28. Aristotle, *Nicomachean Ethics* 1107a.

29. A. H. Armstrong, *An Introduction to Ancient Philosophy* (Boston, 1963), p. 104.

30. John 1:14.

31. 2 Cor. 4:6.

32. Eph. 4:13.

33. K. J. Foreman, *Romans, 1 Corinthians, 2 Corinthians* (Richmond, 1961), p. 37.

34. *Confession of 1967* I, A, 1.

35. Rom. 8:29.

36. J. Gustafson, *Christ and the Moral Life* (New York, 1968), p. 161.

37. John 13:15.

38. E. g., Luke 22:36–38; John 2:15; cp. Matt. 5:39; 26:52.

39. Matt. 4:2.

40. C. Eliot, ed., *The Harvard Classics* (New York, 1909) 7:208.

41. T. à Kempis, *On the Imitation of Christ* 2, 8, 2; 1, 21, 3.

42. Ibid., 2, 20, 3.

43. Ibid., 1, 1, 5.

44. J. Calvin, *Institutes* 3, 6, 3.

45. Ibid., 4, 12, 20.

46. Ibid., 4, 17, 40.

47. Gustafson, op. cit., p. 181.

48. Luke 5:33; 7:33–34.

49. L. Swidler, "Jesus was a Feminist," *Catholic World* (January 1971), p. 183.

50. Eusebius, *Ecclesiastical History* 6, 8. Later in his *Commentary on Matthew* (15, 3), Origen deplored his act because he realized that it was prompted by Hellenistic asceticism and not by a proper interpretation of Matt. 19:12.

51. Origen, *Romans Homilies* 9.

52. L. H. Gray, "Eunuch," *Encyclopedia of Religion and Ethics* (New York, 1928); H. R. Hays, *The Dangerous Sex* (New York, 1964), p. 106.

53. F. C. Conybeare, *Russian Dissenters* (New York, 1962), pp. 367–68.

54. Matt. 19:12; Matt. 5:29; an exception is E. Renan who interprets this verse as showing that "the Master seems to approve those who would mutilate themselves" in pursuit of celibacy. (*The Life of Jesus* [London, 1927], p. 173.)

55. Paul VI, *Sacerdotalis Caelibatus* 21–22.

56. Augustine, *Of Holy Virginity* 35.

57. Methodius, *Symposium* 7, 3.

58. Chrysostom, *Letters to Theodore* 2, 5.

59. Cf. F. Caballero, *Eli, la España treinta anos ha* (Leipzig, 1881), p. 61.

60. Cf. W. Purcell, ed., *The Resurrection* (Philadelphia, 1966), p. 75.

61. D. Callahan, "Self-Identity in an Urban Society," *Theology Today* 24 (April 1967): p. 38.

62. *Zohar Hadash* 4, 50b; cf. *Yebamoth* 62b.

63. R. Gordis, "Re-Judaizing Christianity," *Center Magazine*, September 1968, p. 15.

64. *Koran* 24:32; cp. 57:27; *Mishkatu* 13, 1; *Hadith* 297.

65. W. R. Hoyt, "Re: 'D. H. Lawrence's Appraisal of Jesus,'" *Christian Century* 88 (1971): 862.

66. C. M. Smith, *How to Become a Bishop Without Being Religious* (New York, 1965), p. 21.

67. Justin, *Apology* 1, 15; Clement, *Miscellanies* 3, 6, 50; J. Dupont, *Mariage et Divorce dans l'Evangile* (Bruges, 1959), pp. 161–222; Q. Quesnell, "Made Themselves Eunuchs for the Kingdom of Heaven," *Catholic Biblical Quarterly* 30 (1968):357–58.

68. Cf. W. E. Phipps, *Was Jesus Married?* (New York, 1970), pp. 89–91; W. F. Albright and C. S. Mann, *Matthew* (New York, 1971), commentary on Matt. 19:11.

69. C. Davis, "Was Jesus Married?" the London *Observer*, March 28, 1971.

70. Purcell, ed., op. cit., pp. 93–94.

71. Luke 4:18; 2 Cor. 3:17.

72. Rom. 14:3, 6, 14.

# INDEX